LIFE IS A GAMBLE

TAEYLON GAULDEN-HODGE

CONTENTS

1. Leaders And Followers — 1
2. Dreams and Aspirations — 4
3. Operation Of Decisions — 10
4. Life Can Be Distracting — 18
5. Accept Changes — 29
6. Positive Thinking — 36
7. Giving Up — 47
8. Decision Making — 59
9. The Way To Achievement — 69
10. Money Train — 76
11. Motivation — 80
12. Judging — 82
13. Existences — 91
14. Emotions — 95
15. Finding Yourself — 102
16. Personality — 107
17. It's Not Where You From But Where You're Headed — 111
18. Taeylon Gaulden-Hodge — 116

1

LEADERS AND FOLLOWERS

Life helps me remember a splendid orange box of Uncle Ben's Ready Rice. Rice isn't uncommon, however it's not the rice itself, rather what the rice does.

Excelling ahead of everyone is similar to a bubbling pot of water. We need to preheat the stove and conform it to things we're not use to or even better, disagree with. The pot of water is the pioneer for this situation and the grains of rice are the devotees. Without the water the rice has no potential. A grain of rice has so much potential however it can't act alone.

An automobile with no gas can't proceed with its assignment as the gas is one of the principle ingredients in the auto.

In the workforce there are an extensive variety of pioneers and supporters. The possibility to a business begins with the pioneers. A large portion of us need to be the bubbling pot of water, the pioneer and the best impact of circumstances. Being the reason for things for the most part start with extraordinary choice making. Our brains are customized to achieve our maximum capacity.

Our ears are on our head to serve the brain. The way our thinking operates will have the greatest effect on our lives. Certain people are a big impact to their surroundings and a huge number of us are blinded by individuals who admire us. Commonly, our surroundings haven't changed for the better in light of the fact that we're the example of what achievement looks like.

For instance, 'a few individuals appreciate us so much so that they won't change until they see an adjustment in us.' Being a pioneer begins when we can oversee ourselves in troublesome circumstances. Somehow, we have to not only be admired, but also be a push for change.

A great amount of people I chat with on a daily are striving to be their own boss. A major blunder will happen if we had a kick off into being a leader before we were prepared to do so. The world takes a gander at pioneers as the supervisor; however a few individuals would prefer not to carry on with the grown-up life as their own particular boss, yet we don't know how to be followers.

Famous singer Akon mentioned, "You have to follow, before you can lead." A leader should be reliable at being a person of impact. In a world loaded with skeptics and adherents, consistency is elusive. For the couple of people that are spurred enough, we're advised to surround ourselves around them. Being around leaders, can help us develop similar habits and push us to be a better version of ourselves. We're fit as long as the great inclinations outweigh the bad inclinations.

Anyone that positively affects our lives can be extremely advantageous. Our prosperity shouldn't be aversion towards each other, but it ought to be inspiration for our spirit. It's not a bad thing to be a follower sometimes, it just depends on who or what we choose to follow. At the point when a man realizes what it's like to follow, they'll additionally know what their supporters need. An awesome role model will give individuals a shadow to look up to.

Our insight is a superb thing to leave on the table for our kindred companions and partners. The way we believe is the directing wheel to our life.

An extraordinary approach to get consideration is to show love. Be adorable and take a companion out to eat or perhaps an extraordinary event and get inside their mind. Talk about thoughts of life and approaches to make change. This motivates the brain.

Assembling considerations gives us more conclusions to dispose of, and more to keep. A straightforward discussion can tell us a great deal about a man.

2

DREAMS AND ASPIRATIONS

The world we live in today is based upon dreams and aspirations without enough individuals to satisfy the objectives.

Have you ever considered how the world would be if not a single individual made a positive choice?

Totally extreme!

We cannot advance without help or motivation. Joel Osteen said, "Sometimes we face difficulties not because we're doing something wrong, but because we're doing something right."

God put the hardest difficulties up for the strongest people who are less likely to abandon a smaller circumstance. God doesn't put his hardest individuals up for the most grounded fights. He makes his toughest individuals get through life's hardest fights.

As I considered this, I remembered Mother Theresa. She said, "I know God will never give me more than I can deal with, I simply wish he didn't believe in me to such an extent."

Some moments we experience in life is spent wondering, why we're there.

Life is sometimes unexplainable which can become our downfall. This is something I have heard repeated again and again, as exhortation. I usually set aside and research things I hear to figure out why I hear those things. I thought, amazing, God anticipated that Mary would have the capacity to handle a great deal. I thought Mother Theresa's quote was an interpretation of a verse in the Bible, that somewhere God guaranteed to never give us more than we could deal with.

Yet as I began scrutinizing it, I understood that isn't true. No place in the Bible does it say God won't give us more than we can deal with. My perception towards the issue is that sometimes we put more stress on ourselves than we can handle. Then we blame God for some of our circumstances and forget he gave us a mind to learn right from wrong.

Truth be told, the inverse is true. We are always confronted with more than we can deal with. If we never came up against more than we could deal with, then there would be no requirement for God. This means that God will pull us through anything, and he is the leader and owner of all existing things.

He knows us and he will put no more on us than we can bear. Presently, I comprehend that people say this to bolster those encountering a hard time, yet it isn't substantial. He didn't make me in my mother's womb and say, "This one here, she is adaptable, she is strong, she can manage Cystic Fibrosis."

No, he considered me to be his adolescent, his creation. He knows each changed quality in my body and he said, "Kid, you will see some faint days; days you won't think you will persist. Take heed in knowing that I have successfully won the battle! I will never forsake you on the cutting edge, I will send my eminent chaperons to settle around you, and on the darkest nights, I promise to take you back to the light. I know you are weak. I know you are harmed, yet I promise that in me you will find the quality to fight. We will conquer this together."

Many times, we perceive the grass is greener on the other side when we aren't knowledgeable enough to see the other side. There have been times throughout my life where I would be extremely furious with my mother for not giving me a chance to assume a part in a specific circumstance; which was not an awful thing, but it was things my eyes wasn't ready for. Then again there were times when I needed to experience things to acknowledge that nothing is wrong with my grass.

In some cases, God brings us down darker streets than our neighbors, to imagine things that aren't part of our neighbor's dynasty. We need to make sense of the essentials before we can settle on legitimate choices. Not taking care of things legitimately can make our path longer. Thinking things through step by step settles our choices significantly.

Persistence can destroy us or help us if we rely upon the certainty of the circumstance. An excessive amount of tolerance may make us miss the first open door or the last.

Life is a progression of characteristic and unconstrained changes, where opposing them just causes stress. Things will act as a burden, which makes us get into specific circumstances we can scarcely control.

As a freshman football player, I was prepared to have experiences in varsity. However, before I could begin to know what they were, I was harmed. I felt like I wouldn't be as skilled the next year and I may no longer be one of the best competitors. I told myself that I wouldn't get left behind by any methods.

There were times my body wouldn't allow me to take a shot at things that I expected to improve. I went through numerous workouts with my team, and soon decided to do those same workouts at home. I discovered more tolerance in my life, and truth be told, I was still an incredible competitor.

This test helped me to believe in myself through any destruction in life. I figured out how to make the best out of the time that is given to me.

Before we work through things, we ought to dependably plan our end goal by setting a due date to reach it. These things keep us moving on the right track. A bulletin with due dates is a considerable measure of inspiration to a man who cherishes what he does.

Goals should be scheduled and written down as a priority. Priorities are a business when they're presented through the proper influence. While working towards achievement, we have to develop tools of our own so that our work is unique. Using tools of our own grabs people's attention, because no one can be a better you, than you.

As a person of wisdom, we have to know life can never go bad moving forward, unless we're moving forward in the wrong direction.

Why accept failure when success is free? The road to success is simple, but long. When people set goals they envision things such as money, materials, or happiness. If you're afraid of failing, you won't take the necessary risks required to achieve your goal. For example, you won't make that important phone call, because you're afraid that you'll be rebuffed. Or you won't quit your dead-end job and start your own business because you're afraid that you might end up without any money.

From various perspectives, this trepidation is significantly more weakening than the apprehension of disappointment. Instead, assume you accomplished something astounding, like huge riches.

If you imagine a scenario where you wound up losing every last bit of it. What then? Would your companions begin acting peculiar? Would your family be jealous?

Such musings (and they're normal) can bring about even a profoundly energetic individual to self-harm.

We should instead conclude that we will be glad and appreciative today and upbeat and thankful later on, regardless of what happens.

Instead of shedding the light on conceivable issues, imagine how brilliant it would be to have the capacity to help your loved ones accomplish their objectives.

3

OPERATION OF DECISIONS

When God has an assignment in our lives, we have to delete things and people out of our circle. I learned through my failures to discipline my emotions. Sometimes this means teaching people how to treat you. It's only right to know when and how to deal with different individuals.

Many times, we think we're making a great decision by deleting people from our circle. Life is short and sometimes things are going to surprise us and occur much faster than we think. Deleting someone from around us is not always a secure decision because you never know who you may need and when you will need them.

Life becomes simple when we distance ourselves from all the negative energy. Albert Einstein mentioned, "We cannot solve our problems with the same thinking we used when we created them." As your life enhances, so will your circle. There are many ways we can distance ourselves from all the negative energy and people.

I distance some of my love ones through a phone call every blue moon. You never know who may be the guy with the fortune cookie or who may leave the earth a lot sooner than you thought. Why have hatred towards someone who could be your reason for success? The person some people hate on may be the person that can help or teach them. Everything and everybody is a lesson to learn from.

Our circle defines us as individuals. The things we say and the people we hang around are the strings that brighten up our personality. The way we think and the way we move can make us a million dollar person. Every decision affects us and the people round us. Surround yourself with people who are in love with your presence. We all need someone to care for us and support us, no matter who we are.

People tend to have relationship goals that seek attention and to feel loved. I learned the first step in finding attention is finding it within myself. We have to fall in love with ourselves before we expect someone else to do the same.

Loving yourself will bring things like happiness and success towards you. Sometimes we ask ourselves 'why me?', 'who am I to be a legend?', and the response is, *who am I not to be a legend.*

We are God's children; no person is better than the

next. The things that make life brighter, starts with decision making.

A man once asked me, "What is success?"

When a person reaches their goals and finds happiness, they'll find success. We all work out a little, study a little, and we expect this big fortune after we're done. In order to earn an A+ you have to prepare for an A+.

Most people prepare or study just to succeed. Success has no limitation. Many times we limit ourselves because of the doubt we have towards our capability. Too much doubt, can stop us from living our lives to the fullest.

Some people can never make up their minds about their careers, their love lives or much else. These things lead people to expect too much credit for not enough work.

The problem is that we can never really know what the outcome of our decisions will be. That's the nature of life. But the people who never take a risk, however small, get nowhere.

At some point, after a little looking, you've got to leap. In order to be on top, you have to outwork the people around you. Outworking somebody sometimes means staying up through midnight preparing for the future, knowing we have to be at work in the morning.

People will go overboard to be on top if they want it bad enough. In this lifetime, in order to be on top, our results should motivate us to reach higher and not just be satisfied.

For example, if a sports team only practiced a little, they will not be the best. Athletes throw up at practice, experience body cramps, and pass out every day just to be champions and at the end of the season. There is only one champion. The most important thing is giving you an opportunity.

At the age of ten, I started reading the bible consistently and working on my football skills. During this process, the best of my football ability began to show. This was one experience that showed me anything can be done.

But life gets a lot more difficult than my experience. In fact, I've witnessed many parents mention things like feeding and providing for their kids. We as people, will sometimes glorify ourselves for the things that we are supposed to do.

For instance, cooking, cleaning, going to school, working two jobs, providing for our kids, and more. Because you are attentive to self-glory, you will work to get greater glory even when you aren't aware that you're doing it. You will tend to tell personal stories that make you the hero. You will find ways, in public settings, of talking about private acts of faith. Because you think you're worthy of acclaim, you will seek the acclaim of others by finding ways to present yourself as "godly."

The thing that we are supposed to do doesn't make

our thinking better than the next, because they are mandatory. You often hear, you need to prioritize your work to be more effective. You may even believe you are one person who can prioritize very well. But think again, how much do you get completed in a day? Do you leave work feeling you have done a lot, but realize more needs to be done? Do you confuse what you do as business while all you have been doing is *busyness*?

What is the difference you ask? One is doing what the work truly entails and needs. That is business. The other is doing all sorts of activities that make you look busy but hardly makes an impact on your career or even project.

Many times I've questioned why our parents and love ones do not push us to be a Senator, famous doctor, author, actress, etc. And the only answer that comes to mind is that our love ones only believe in us to a certain extent. People tend to not have a lot of faith in things they haven't witnessed.

Many families that we see daily have never witnessed their friends winning the jumbo pot or becoming famous. These are things that people spend most of their lives dreaming about. Many people believe in things that they wouldn't support or try, that are much higher than the goals they are aiming for in the same field, because they're slightly doubting the fact.

Instead of getting better at things that will bring success, we brag about priorities. Proud people tend to talk about themselves a lot. I've met individuals who think no one has experienced the great things they've experienced in life. Or no one has had the laughs or good times they've had in life. Proud people tend to like their opinions more than the opinions of others. Many people think their way is the best way, and their thinking is the best thinking.

Proud people think their stories are more interesting and engaging than others. There are some people who are stuck in their ways and believe there is absolutely nothing wrong with their choices.

Many people think they know and understand more than others. Some will confuse haters and criticize with the truth. Individuals can be so stuck on themselves that they will overlook their blessings.

At times we will never know what we need until we need it; however, it can be too late by that time. Individuals think they've earned the right to be heard. Many times, our success doesn't apply to another person that is less fortunate. Everyone knows instinctively what they want, but not as much of what they need. When all your needs are taken care of, your wants will fall into place.

Proud people, because they are basically proud of what they know and what they've done, talk a lot about both. Proud individuals don't reference weakness. Proud love ones don't talk about failure. Proud people don't confess sin. So proud individuals are better at putting the spotlight on them than they are at shining the light of their stories and opinions on God's glorious and utterly undeserved grace.

Sometimes you will see friends and family fail over and over again until success is their last opportunity. Proud people sometimes mislead the less fortune by speaking from the wrong point of view as if they're Gods or what not. We have to humble ourselves and put ourselves in a position to motivate others without criticizing them.

Some of you may be surprised that items that are important but not urgent are more crucial than items that are urgent but not important. The reason is when you procrastinate on the important but not urgent, it eventually catches up to be in the important and urgent column.

So, before it catches up, do it first. From my understanding, we're supposed to learn from situations and people so we don't put ourselves in a position of regret. At times we are so admired by our talent we forget there was room for improvement, which can possibly lead to failure. God usually shows us the way out before we leave ourselves trapped in.

Sometimes we don't want to hear others' opinions that can change our lives or our thinking. I have family and friends that will argue a situation to the best of their ability before they even give the situation an opportunity. You trust your opinions, so you are not as interested in the opinions of others as you should be. You will tend to want your thoughts, perspectives, and viewpoints to win the day in any given meeting or conversation.

This means you will be way more comfortable than you should be with dominating a gathering with your talk. You will fail to see that in a multitude of counsel, there is wisdom. You will fail to see the essential ministry of the body of Christ in your life. You will fail to recognize your bias and spiritual blindness. So you come to meetings, formal or informal with a personal sense of need for what others have to offer, and you will control the talk more than you should.

My grandfather once said to me, "you have two ears and one mouth for a reason." I had to suffer and go through many things to realize this statement applied to me heavily. The craziest thing is, once I heard this statement, I shouldn't of had to go through things to realize this applied to me, but I wasn't listening.

As a kid we tend to hear things and confuse them with the thought of listening. Sometimes we cheat ourselves by not accepting help or advice. Our pride can sometimes be our biggest downfall. Once we as individuals get our mind productively on the right track, our needs will slim and our wants will vary. Therefore, most of us will go to a higher level of thinking and positively referring to the obstacles of our needs. If we as people of the world put our priorities first, we wouldn't have to find our wants; they will find us.

4

LIFE CAN BE DISTRACTING

I was examining an arrangement with one of my relatives about the reason they abandoned a clothing line that they were working towards. During the discussion, I acknowledged that he surrendered his goal because he wasn't sufficiently accepting of the results.

I've always believed that anything is possible. Now, I'm not going to tell you I haven't abandoned a couple of circumstances, however I gained a lot from any circumstance that I've abandoned. The clothing line, one of my relatives attempted to start, led to individuals putting requests on shirts that they later couldn't pay for or decided they didn't want anymore.

My uncle, the owner of the clothing line, ended up having to spend more cash on shirts than he was for making the shirts.

I thought this was really funny, not because I didn't

want him to succeed, but rather because he didn't even give his clothing line time to grow.

While viewing the film *'Are We Done Yet',* The main character thought the renovation of his home would be a snappy procedure. He became very angry when he saw his home going into disrepair while they were chipping away at things in the house. His wife said to him, "Baby, don't stress. Things need to end up monstrous, before they can turn out to be lovely."

Things go to pieces before they can fall together. Breakdowns can make leaps through breakthroughs.

In fact, you hear it constantly, individuals winding up in a sorry situation before their business can take off. It's hard to compose another story on a sheet of paper effectively secured with words, yet if you're given a spotless sheet of paper, a fresh start, it's much simpler to make whatever story you'd like. You need to make space for the new by freeing yourself of the old.

Lamentably, when things truly go into disrepair for a man, they have a tendency to feel completely overwhelming. Staying positive when your reality is disintegrating around you is no simple assignment. Yet, you will see that each negative thing that happened, happened with an end goal that will show you that you can turn your life around.

Sometimes, life will appear to be great and reasonable to you. Different times it will appear to be out of line, harboring cold-blooded goals. What you need to recall is that life itself is neither reasonable nor out of line; it basically is whatever it is.

There is no malevolent being out there attempting to make things troublesome for you, attempting to out you with the goal that you bumble and fall. Individuals may attempt to cut you down, however not even life itself can do so.

Many individuals end up deploring over their own incidents, asking the sky for what good reason they were so unfortunate, requesting that they did merit what they accept to be a discipline. Be that as it may, nobody is rebuffing you. Every once in a while, awful things happen to great individuals. It sucks, yet it's the truth of things. You can't thrash yourself for it. You need to do your best to hold yourself together and keep pushing forward.

In your lifetime, you will encounter misfortune. You will experience distress, tragedy, torment, and enduring. The amount of each can be an opportunity to choose. However, you are prone to encounter a bit of each to some degree or another.

I'm sure of this as it truly happens to everybody. Each individual lives these negative encounters; there is no special case. Your encounters will doubtlessly vary from those of others, however, the torment is just about the same. You may be uncommon, yet not in such a manner. Everyone endures. Everyone loses. Many will surrender. Many will acknowledge rout. Be that as it may, some will discover the quality to continue pushing, continue attempting, and continue imagining. At the point when things go into disrepair for you, which they likely will at some point in your life, you will have a decision you'll have to make. You can either flounder in your adversities or you can choose that such a destiny is unsatisfactory. You have the ability to decline rout. You have the quality to withstand each and every blow. No matter what, you need to stay standing. You need to examine your circumstance and choose without even a moment's pause that you are going to roll out improvements, and that you are going to turn things around for yourself because you merit better.

The world gets upside down because we're easily satisfied without enough results. Things that fall apart before they become better usually leave us satisfied without enough results. We're nothing without our results. Rather, we're trying to get a job or a starting position on the football field. I've learned over the years to affiliate myself with the perfect pleasure of reaching my goals.

Companions that are aiming for perfection themselves rub the right sort of information on us. Pleasure is a piece of affection and aspiration, which gives us the audacity to appreciate the opposition in front of us. Sometimes we have to enjoy our journey in order to earn our destination. Pleasure is something that has dependably kept individual's eyes on the prize. Love can grab on to us in many of ways.

Distraction is easy to stumble into. Commonly, we have confidence in ourselves until we see things getting harder before they turn out to be better. Friends and technology can get the best of our attention. A wise man once said to me, "if you stop believing, you'll fail".

Publicity goes on every day of the week and distracts people in the classroom and on the highways. While hearing things about celebrities and spending our time speaking about their actions, we're destroying our own time. Celebrities' income will increase the more the world speaks about them despite the good or bad. Publicity has become one of the biggest distractions of all time. Me and a few friends have acknowledged that the moments we waste our time and money, were usually benefiting someone else. For instance, every time we go buy a pair of shoes that we don't need, we're hurting ourselves and benefiting the owner of the shoes and the business that provided the shoes.

We're all trying to be unique to the wrong eyes and voices. Everyone is posting the same quotes and complaining about the same things. Why hasn't anything changed? We're all trying to look independent and sophisticated to people who aren't independent or sophisticated. In today's society, I see too many talkers and not enough listeners trying to impress the people instead of keeping our eyes on the prize; which may put you in a drought that's difficult to tolerate.

I'm not a big Facebook fan because I see many people trying so hard to let others know they're working towards success without a definite purpose. When I was eleven years old, I used to speak to people about how talented I would be when I became older. A man stopped me and said it's better to surprise people with your work than to notify them that entertainment is coming.

Things are going to fall apart with or without a million dollars. The world is ours and success is free. Talking and listening in a balanced way are crucial in our reality. Listening will lead us to procedures we're unfamiliar with. The confusion of pointless words that a hefty portion of us are using for another person's consideration makes a thick haze that doesn't allow for us to understand one another.

Amusingly, the more we talk, the less we're ready to impart. I love to generate my results to other people to emphasize that anything can be accomplished. Sometimes I find myself getting upset about not being able to get things done in a decent amount of time. I've told myself as long as I have completed my assignment today, I'm moving forward.

While starting a business, things are going to get out of hand and we are not to let go or become distracted. Distraction can come from listening to the wrong people or not listening at all. We have to visualize the path that people are trying to send us down, no matter if we like that path or not.

As a country, we are behind in business, reading, and other things because of many distractions and lazy people. Lazy people, as in people who are satisfied very easily or people that want to search for jobs but let the government take care of their home. For example, churches are marrying gay couples, which is just as unexplainable as praising two Gods.

How do we even let this be allowed in our country? How are men going to be leaders to their sons? It's very difficult to understand how gay men can control a household or be role models to their sons. How are gay women going to be queens to their daughters? A few friends told me it doesn't matter because of the separation of church and state.

The problem is how do we expect God to lead our marriage if he never approved it in the first place. What makes it right to do all the things God is not pleased with and then call on his name? There is nothing that makes it right; it creates distractions and misunderstanding. This country is built under God. We mention it in our pledge. The best way to get God's attention is to obey him. I figure we're losing justice in America. When we are surrounded by things that aren't right and things that will fall apart, we begin to fall apart.

I told my father as a little boy that I would love to

use my left hand just as much as my right hand and he told me you will have to first make using your left hand a habit. We're creatures of habit. It becomes our behavior. Life is measured in moments. At times, it appears that for the same number of hours there are in the day, there are three times the same number of interferences that detract you from work that needs to be completed. So, what would you be able to do to get somewhat more clarity and dispose of those diversions?

Music gets in the way of a lot of things, especially Hip-Hop. It makes certain people feel lame if they've never sold dope or put a person in critical condition. A white man once said to me if a person can make you pursue actions in your life that they've experienced or want you to think they've experienced that will lead you down the wrong road, how does that make you a man.

The world will change when we as individuals change to become better. The measure of data we soak in on occasions in our mind may not be utilized. We have all these new advancements which are great at diverting us, which our human propensities have not made up for lost time to. The test is that we have not understood the genuine expense of diversions; they go through what is really a constrained supply of consideration every day and make us far less viable on the off chance that we have to do more profound speculation work. Each time you center your consideration, you utilize a quantifiable measure of glucose and other metabolic assets.

Studies show that every assignment you do makes you less compelling at the following errand, and this is valid for high-vitality undertakings like discretion or choice making. You're grinding away; highly involved with handling a venture that requires extraordinary core interest. You're having some fantastic luck. You're in the zone. And afterward your telephone rings, snapping you out of your stream. It's only a telemarketer, so the call takes only a moment. Then you check your email, your Facebook, take a gander at your Twitter channel and before you know it, you've chosen your companion.

When you at last return to work two, five, possibly 10 minutes after the beginning interference, it's harder to concentrate. You delay checking your email once more, examine the local news and take a gander at adorable little cat pictures on Instagram. Thusly, you end up committing more errors. In the event this sounds natural, you're a long way from alone. Sadly, our brains are finely sensitive to diversion and even the briefest ones have the ability to hinder our efficiency. You shouldn't stretch the actuality in light of the fact that even the best and decided individuals let things divert them. It's part of our human instinct.

Growing up, we were told to go to college and get a degree. We take math classes that have nothing to do with our career and students feel the teachers are making them do unnecessary studies. Whenever we're pursuing something that we seem to think is unnecessary, we do not give our best towards that subject. We become distracted and annoyed with math because we've never seen our parents use most of the methods that we are told to learn. Many times, people that are very picky about their job are great at what they do. While solving a math problem, the smallest mistake can make a big difference in your final outcome.

Hypothetically speaking, math is always 100% correct when solved using the proper techniques. For example, while solving a math problem, if your final answer appears to be 53 and you make an error and fill in -53 and the teacher marks it wrong, you feel that the teacher is being petty. We also will think this is a small mistake. However, if you arrive at the bank and learn that your balance is -$5,000 because of a small mistake, you will feel that it is an enormous mistake. Math is made to develop us into precise workers. The subject of math has troubled many people, as it is easy to misunderstand the concepts.

Science and math are used in most job fields and careers. Many say science is common sense. The facts and tools of science are accurate depending on the dependability of the situation. Over many years, I've learned that science is important in the medical field. Albert Einstein said, "education is not the learning of facts, but the training of the mind to think."

Literature develops us into being better speakers and thinkers. Essays and class articles provide us with creativity and imagination. Imagination can be worth so many benefits when you seek ways of exploring your styles and producing it in unique ways. Creativity is one of the most amazing gifts a person can develop. Maybe if we understand ways that train our mind to think; subjects won't distract us as much.

5

ACCEPT CHANGES

While going to Piedmont hospital in Stockbridge, Georgia, I was waiting in the hallway with a sweetheart of mine across from a therapeutic room. There was a man in the room with his life partner and he was continually going in and out of the room chatting with us like he'd known us for years. He had a stunning comical inclination and was a minding man.

We were waiting in the hallway, waiting to be seen for no less than four hours. While we waited, the man ordered a pizza and offered us some, however we declined. Not long after this, the specialist took my companion to run tests on her to see what the issue was. When she returned to the hallway to sit with me and wait on her results, the fellow that offered us pizza said, "hey me and my life partner are about to be dismissed; you folks better hustle just a bit and consume this space before another person does." We were sitting in the lobby because we thought every one of the rooms in the emergency room were taken.

My sweetheart was discussing Wendy's chili throughout the day. Even the medical aids were saying to make sure I buy her some chili after we were discharged. They were great specialists by the way. I reacted to them, saying perhaps that is the reason her stomach is having issues.

I got disappointed staying there, and the specialist said, "Well if she didn't need any chili, we would be the ones that know." The gentleman that requested pizza said something to us again. He said, "I know you all are ready to be discharged. You all have been here awhile". As the medical aids were discharging his life partner he said to me, "Come up out of that. Today is not about you, it's about her. You have been doing great staying here holding up with her now. You may need a few kisses this evening. Go purchase her some chili".

The medical aids took extraordinary consideration of us and offered us sustenance as they were discharging us with no dithering. Every one of the janitors, therapeutic helps, security officers, and patients said to us, "You folks have an awesome night and keep in mind to purchase her some stew," with enormous astounding grins on their faces.

I was truly stuck in my zone and didn't acknowledge the way that my better half was in pain and truly needed her chili. I eventually wound up taking her to Wendy's that night after I saw her getting upset.

We as people, become stuck in our ways and have an excessive amount of pride. The vast majority of us like to be in recognizable settings and work inside known circumstances. It makes us feel more secure.. Fundamentally we turn out to be so OK with our propensities until we start to believe they're alright to proceed with or we're frightened to alter in light of the fact that we think, *hey! I'm really one of a kind and clever individuals adore me*.

There is something about all doctor's facilities that I disdain with enthusiasm. I make a decent attempt to maintain a strategic distance from them, yet the day my sweetheart was in pain, it was difficult to stay away from a healing center. I'm not in my comfort zone inside a doctor's facility and I have an issue being persistent about things. I concede this is totally childish. The awesome thing is I really attempt to improve and take my issues and egotistical approaches to God.

I've figured out how to change my reasoning and acknowledge the way that even if something was precise yesterday, it doesn't mean it will dependably be exact tomorrow. In some cases, we as individuals make it hard to attempt new things. We take in data and lock it into our way to deal with the world. Regardless of that, this data might become obsolete or even be inaccurate. Once we bolt onto it, it for the most part, stays put. Individuals are frequently afraid to not be right, to admit mistakes. Indeed, even with learning new truths, individuals hold to their convictions. Better to hold on to outdated convictions than to admit to being wrong.

I've met people who would tell me in the middle of an inspirational conversation, "I don't care about that I'm not changing for nobody." Okay, let's face reality. It is one thing changing for people and it's another thing changing for the better. Change is hard. There is security in doing the same things again and again.

"Imagine a scenario in which I reacted to it terribly. I had a relative of mine say to me, "let me show you the correct approach dribble a basketball." I would always say, "man move out my way, I know how to dribble a basketball."

Most of my life I grew up believing I could dribble a basketball when other people thought different. So, one day, I decided I would sit back and listen. It took my relative two minutes to literally teach me how to dribble a basketball. The worst feeling about this is I had already let my basketball career go. I was done with basketball, but years and years before that I would've been a much better basketball player if I would've only taken two minutes out to listen.

Being stuck in our ways can ruin a lot of things God has planned for us if we don't let them go sooner rather than later. We feel as if we're being criticized or have haters. Albert Einstein said, "We cannot solve our problems with the same thinking we used when we created them."

Old ways need to open to new entryways. We need to change courses and find other way, if it's not going right. The initial phase in pushing ahead is acknowledging you will win and other times you will learn. Mix-ups are made just to set up the psyche for better.

Henry Ford said, "Failure is the only opportunity to begin again, only this time more wisely." As we make mistakes, we're becoming a better person only if we learn from them. For example, when choosing a university, a person may make a poor choice because of misleading or confusing course descriptions, or because the brain failed to remember which college had the best ratings.

Sometimes not making mistakes can be our biggest mistake. With every mistake that we make, we discover more and more about ourselves, about who we are, about our limits, about our capabilities, about what we can and cannot do. They help us be more compassionate and more tolerant with ourselves and others. One of the greatest lessons you will learn from making mistakes is forgiveness. With every mistake that you make, you learn how important it is to forgive yourself and many of the people around you. You understand that you are not perfect and that perfection doesn't exist, only our intentions of doing your best.

And who wants to be perfect, anyway? Perfection leaves no room for improvement.

Many of my mistakes have shaped me into a monster when it comes down to work ethic. Becoming a go-getter inspires the people around you and they will inspire the people around them. We can be the reason for everyone's improvement, but we should always remember we were sent by God. Some people will fail from using our ways and our knowledge because what's meant for you will not always benefit everyone else. Sometimes we fail, not because we weren't ready, but because we weren't ready enough.

Faith is a small thing that's very challenging. Many people believe in God but don't have faith in him. All God expects from us is faith as small as a watermelon seed.

As a person of interest, I simply love to surprise people with the output of my dreams. Surprising our peers with a great output of our hard work will only inspire them and leave us room to talk about future preferences. Talk is cheap while hard work is expensive. Humble yourself and accept changes. By doing this, you will change circumstances and people around you. Sometimes all you need to accept a change is to forget it. Try pampering yourself, have a hot bath, play some games, do some meditating, anything to keep your mind off what you changed. Mistakes can occur rapidly because we accept changes.

I have many positive things floating through my

mind, so I usually look for a creative way to share these things with people. Many times, in order to get attention from others, you have to give others what they haven't seen or witnessed from anyone else. Some individuals have positive things to say, but many people don't have the effect to touch people with those same words. The way we use our minds can be a big key during a motivational speech.

Creativity is a small thing with big opportunities, but the opportunity gets bigger the more creative we become. Opportunities are the worst thing to let slip away. I've come across individuals who would say, "What if the opportunity comes back around?" I always respond with, "What if that was your season?"

Growing up, I've had a few obstacles in my way. I always thought, maybe I should lay down or maybe I should jump over them, but what if my legs are broken? However, I should train my legs and stay ahead of some of my components. Once my legs are all healed up, I'm still a part of the competition because I never quit. Let's just say if you don't discipline your downfalls, you can easily paralyze your opportunities. Try to get used to the new thing you gained to replace the old with. You might find out you like it more.

6

POSITIVE THINKING

I love Football. I remember when I was eight years old, my community didn't have a football division for my age group. I cried and cried consistently and asked my granddad to play on his football team, while he was coaching the eleven and twelve-year-old children. He said to me again and again, "Child your time is coming. I'm not permitted to do that, and those young men are much stronger and bigger than you." I genuinely couldn't care less how enormous they were. I simply wanted to play. I would wear my uncle's football gear around the house and toss the football all around, playing without anyone else's input. By one means or another, my affection for football grew and I would eat with my uncle's shoulder pads on.

The high school football players in the community were my legends. I would imagine I was them while playing football in the house. A few weeks after football season began, I moved to Columbus, Georgia and attended Martin Luther King Elementary. My mother, sister, and I had little family members in Columbus, so I had to go directly to the boys and girls' club after school because I had no babysitter. One of the football coaches at the boys and girls' club walked up to me and said, "you look like an athlete. Do you want to join our flag football team?" I was a little happy but not very happy because I wanted to wear football pads like high school players. I attended practice for a few days and played in one game.

After my first game, I quit the team. I told my mom they were boring, and I wanted to tackle somebody. The very next year I was living in Fitzgerald, Georgia again and was old enough to play tackle football. In fact, my first run of the season was the first play of the game and I gained a lot of yards. The fans were hyped thinking I was about to score. I was an amazing athlete throughout my little league football career, which led to the same results while playing middle school football.

My seventh-grade year was my first year ever playing football for our middle school; I was a key player on our team. My eighth-grade year, however, was a disaster. Individuals were expecting huge things out of me, so their expectations influenced me not to make excuses. I continued to do my best and play hard while I was injured. Listening to others tell me to toughen up, only made my condition worse. I started the season remarkably, playing extremely well in our first two games. Out of the blue, I had hip pain that kept me from being the competitor I could be. I would get called out my name by coaches since I couldn't perform the way they needed me to. Individuals would tell me, "nothing is wrong with you, you're just not tough." I would hear my companions rehash again and again. Mind over matter. Toughen up.

From my understanding, it's not difficult to single out somebody when you're on the outside looking in. I likewise came across very honest individuals that were exceptionally chivalrous that would let me know, "if you're hurt, you're hurt. There is nothing you can do about it."

Wait, a second! Shouldn't something be said about the folks that said excuses are for failures? We should take a deep breath and take this into consideration.

Well, I expected on the off chance that if it's powerful to you, you'll find a way. Finding a way is settling the issue the best way available. Finding excuses mostly breaks into a channel. For example, the water we used to give today will just satisfy us for the moment. Excuses are normally made for the occasion; they more often than not avoid obligation on to circumstances and peers.

The circumstance I confronted through my harm lead me to not having the capacity to be a varsity starter my first year of high school. Truth be told, I wound up sitting out the entire season. I was continually going to specialists and advisors to see what was wrong and nobody had a piece of information.

I wound up going to Tifton, Georgia to get a shot from a male specialist who seemed as though he was seven feet tall. He was an extraordinary specialist and jabbed me in my hip with a needle. I haven't had any issues with my hip since that day. I would do push-ups, sit-ups, toe raises and those sorts of things, while my hip was pestering me. While doing the things to improve as a competitor that my body allowed me to do, I improved massively, while others thought differently. During the time I wasn't playing, I had the option to sit around and complain instead of doing what my body allowed me to.

If your car is having issues, what might be your best arrangement? I accept that one answer for this would be to settle it yourself. Many people start feeling sorry for themselves and expect others to do the same. I've seen men replace screws with tape and rubber bands. Some might say, "gosh what an idiot," however, in the event that it worked, you're a genius.

When it comes to something we really love, we hop right on things that would attach us to that thing or person. Why do we look online for the puzzles and pieces to connect a trampoline together, but we will make an excuse if our car doesn't crank? My thoughts towards this condition are that it's very possible to fix it ourselves. Of course, we have to figure out what's causing the issue.

Now you may think I'm going a bit overboard, but I'm more than sure a person can find the solution to any car issue online.

I understand, a car is on a totally different level. Some may say, what if I don't have the tools? Well walking, catching the train, buying tools, borrowing tools or catching the bus is also an option. I'm not telling you to be a fool, but weigh your options.

Well, the transmission is different because by the time you've hoisted the engine out of the way or done whatever else, you've spent enough labor to make it feasible to just rebuild the whole thing. If you have recurring excuses, it is a good thing to learn them.

I've recognized in recent years all guidance isn't for our motivation, regardless if the announcement was valid. For instance, push-ups will make most individuals stronger while it can harm someone who's handicap. A few people, gatherings, partnerships, and more can give us a standout amongst the most rousing talks ever. However, the vast majority of them can't describe their words.

I've been told a couple times to do as I say and not as I do. My dear Lord wouldn't pick a minister to lead a congregation that is experiencing the opposite of what he's proclaiming. In today's reality, "practice what you preach" is a well-known quote. As far as anyone is concerned, this shows me why my nation doesn't have the same number of genuine leaders as individuals claim to be.

Everyone appears to have an incredible mouthpiece in my generation, brimming with investigating tones and breathtaking decision of words. Most of these shocking words are from online networking clients who are a portion of the greatest persuasive speakers that don't carry on with the way of life they're lecturing. In addition, a leader can't lead without his activities. We're continually advising our children to lead with their actions while they're seeing us lead with our voices. When we lead the wrong way, we give our child the option to blame us for their downfalls. A kid would be told they're disrespectful when they take after our negative activities, yet not our positive speaking words. However, this is awful parenting regardless of how we attempt to sum it up using an essentialness sense of knowledge.

This is similar to a chief or a man chastising us for breaking the same guidelines they're breaking. However, it's very clear individuals respect our activities more than our voices. The world could be improved if individuals try to do what they say others should do. By one means or another, many people don't try to do what they say others should do, which prompts excuses.

This is a huge issue in America. How could we settle these things? How about we simply begin by saying what you believe is correct, is not always right, or the most ideal way. Excuses are often made to shift blame away to circumstances beyond our control.

Many times, again and again, we appear to work things out using the wrong thought process. Some say marijuana can hurt us, some say differently. Be that as it may, that is not my point.

Liquor and tobacco are absolutely executing our residents, however, it's still lawful. The most ideal approach to elevate the peripheral part of a circumstance is to check whether the great exceeds the terrible. There is no compelling reason to work things lawfully that have a negative resistance. I catch my companions saying, "Get the lawbreakers off the avenues and improve the world." I don't think lawbreakers are truly the issue. Once a man carries out a wrongdoing in America, your decisions turn out to be more constrained, which shows chances to blur away.

The thing is, this aggravates circumstances because of further notice since individuals need to sustain themselves, regardless. These things will prompt individuals to do negative things to nourish them and their family. No, I'm not saying it's alright but they're being captured by officers, and are being sentenced by individuals that don't battle to nourish their homes.

At the point when a man doesn't comprehend what it's like to struggle, it's really hard to comprehend a man that is struggling. There are different approaches to handle pardons, yet how would we think quickly when it's a great opportunity to respond fast. What might we do on the off chance that we had no gifts offered or a vocation supplying a wage and we were starving?

Many individuals are humble and great decision makers until they're tossed into extreme circumstances that prompt them assessing a wrongdoing. What's wrong will be wrong and shouldn't be done. There are relatively few who will simply endure and pass on.

Why not make the right choices? I think there should be commercials for lawbreakers and welfare natives with things that will offer them some assistance with a superior answer for each issue. The starting stride to stopping excuses is to review the sum you consider life to be being in your control. Our exercises, we can control. We can stand up and guarantee ourselves with self-thought, or we can allow it to take us away.

While facing injuries and watching individuals around me suffer, God has still permitted me to accept there is no time for excuses. We were talking about criminals improving their lives mostly because they're the ones that are typically enduring the most because of unemployment. At the point when God is prepared for somebody to change and settle on better choices, he will permit things to transpire that will not eliminate their chance to do better.

There was a period on this planet when enduring and distress did not exist. At the point when God initially made man upon the earth, everything was great. There was no affliction, no torment, and no distress of any sort. It was God's arrangement for man to live in peace and congruity, never experiencing distress. By part three, it wasn't until man picked the method for Satan, instead of the method for God, that distress entered the world. God told Adam and Eve that they would now encounter distress and demise. In this way, the affliction and distress that you and I confront today is not the work of an unfair God; it's the result of sin. We endure in light of the fact that we are miscreants. The wages of sin are passing, yet we will always live for Jesus.

You might say, "I didn't do anything incorrectly. Why am I a miscreant?" We are all conceived with a wrongdoing nature. Maybe you are thinking, "What's the point? What does God achieve by permitting us to suffer?"

Basically, He's attempting to let us know something. By permitting individuals to endure, God is demonstrating to us that something is wrong. In the event that everything was okay in the middle of man and God, then there would be no distress and demise, in light of the fact that before all else, there was none.

God is demonstrating to you each day of your life that man has been separated from him in view of sin, and that man is bound to an unfathomable length of time in hell fire unless he comes to God for help. The way that God allows suffering and desolation today demonstrates that He will permit it endlessness, too.

God doesn't enjoy seeing anybody struggle, yet he allows individuals to suffer for different reasons. On the off chance that you've never confirmed the Lord Jesus Christ as your Savior, then God needs you to see your need to do such. In some cases, God needs to permit tragedies to enter someone's life, keeping in mind the end goal to inspire somebody to look to Him for Salvation. As somebody has said, "A few individuals won't admire God until he puts them on their back." This is miserable, yet genuine.

There are many individuals who might at present be lost in their wrongdoings if God had not brought some tragedies into their life to stand out enough to be noticed. As a child, I would always get asked by individuals, what I needed to do with my life. I figured they were simply verifying whether my head was progressing nicely. I would announce to everybody that I would prefer not to be rich. I simply need to be fruitful, or I don't need ten cars. I'll take three. However, my life isn't about the cash, yet some of my answers weren't the best. I feel I wasn't thinking as large as I ought to have been thinking, until I was dependably enamored with Jesus Christ and he permitted me to encompass myself around individuals who were thinking greater, which made me think greater.

I didn't have the best life and neither did I have the

worse life growing up, however individuals around me would settle in light of their pride. My faculties dependably instructed me to take the first way out. Simply pondering internally, I understood that my pride can later transform into excuses. It's very easy to remain a failure when you don't have a chance, said a criminal. I totally agree and disagree because every day is a chance to become better, but I wouldn't keep doing things that would put me in a deeper hole.

7

GIVING UP

As a young child, I grew up with a single parent. No, this is not a dramatization or a complaint. I never understood the genuine importance of a single parent until I became mature enough to understand.

My dad was somewhere using the best excuses on the planet. Truly, he was astonishing with his reasons. He was the kind of man that would make me feel frustrated about his reasons.

Not having my dad around also profited me in many ways. In any case, I would try to do everything my mother did for me, with no excuse for my children. As a man, I believe it's great to accomplish for your children what most moms accomplish for their children.

I cherish great parents by signing papers and giving them my last. Some say we as children are unappreciative. Maybe we are in a way. I believe we're more spoiled than anything. It's kind of our parent's fault, yet they probably wouldn't admit it. I rarely ever ask myself how my life would have been if I had my father around. Maybe because the more tragedies throughout my life, the better the story is in the end. The story is fascinating at the point where we're able to pull through and land on top.

I'm currently following the light God has sparkled for me. Each stride I take, appears as though the light becomes brighter. As a child, I didn't feel success until I became closer to the Lord. I'm not yet a Christian, but I fear God more every day, which keeps me from doing a ton of things that I would have done in the past.

I remember growing up; I used to tell my loved ones I want an enormous house with a major fence around my yard. Nobody told me any of the strains and battles that it would take to accomplish my dream. They helped keep my head on the right path by telling me it was possible, however they didn't lie.

I'm assuming these individuals left out the most critical thing that I needed to know in order to achieve my goals, so that I kept my confidence. The most vital thing was the battles that I would face to get there. Perhaps I would've taken school more seriously or wouldn't have taken school as seriously.

Sometimes I wonder about the things that I was not told, but the thing is if I know now, I still have no excuse. Despite all the tragedies we go through as individuals, I am grateful for them because life would be pointless without trials and tribulations.

I'm steadily affirming myself with determination and confidence. Your determination can begin from a state of weakness in your circumstances. You can also form a conscious decision to run with the best option that is accessible under your circumstances. Self-confident individuals are respected and inspire confidence in others. They face their apprehensions head-on and have a tendency to be risk takers. They realize that regardless of what obstructions come their direction, they can get past them. Individuals that don't trust in themselves will surrender effortlessly in intense fights.

While sitting in class at Morehouse University, an inspiring man spoke at the assembly, informing the students about a time he was riding in the car with his children. His children had found a piece of candy and asked their father to take a bite. The father said while he was biting the candy, he found that the candy was bitter and hard. His children saw the expression all over his face. He began to spit the candy out, but his children said, no dad, you just need to continue chewing again and again until you get to the sweet part.

Whenever we experience what it's like to go through the struggle and find the sweet part of life, we'll always believe in ourselves.

My first year of spring football practice was the

start of my sophomore season in high school. I had an amazing spring game running all over the place, making football look very easy. No matter what I did it seemed as if the more I did the further I would get pushed back from being a starter. Later that summer, I would go outside every night and do jump-ropes to improve my stamina. The beginning of fall came around and we had a game called the soap game. This game required all fans and supporters to bring soap in order to enter the game. Many fans expressed their thoughts, that I played fairly well this game. Somehow, I still ended up not having a starting position.

At the beginning of the season, I started off playing extremely well with the first big run of the season. I also scored on my first touch.

I would go to practice and get chewed out constantly about the little things I didn't do right. Many times my coach would find another reason why I didn't start when I handled the previous problem.

The thing is, I never gave up. I came to a point in the season where no one could tackle me at practice. I was running the ball in a beast mode attitude tempting the coaches to award me scout team player of the week back to back. My coaches were also new coaches that transferred from different schools, so they didn't have much film to see on me from the previous year. However, I never got that starting position that I went through trials and tribulations for.

Our defense had no major problems from stopping

any running-backs in a football game. They always seemed to get the job done. Despite all of that, I somehow found confidence during the season.

I knew I had the ability and the potential, but once I found confidence, I found determination. Learning is a tool you can never disgrace. Let's learn to love the competition and enjoy the battles.

Life is a game of chess. Reasoning well, about complicated problems required recognizing patterns, structures, and analogies so the situation could be isolated into simpler pieces.

Women are powerful in many forms and situations. The queen is the most powerful piece on the board, the king, by contrast, is plodding and slow. The game goes on and on through several moves until the king dies.

In life, women are the center of attention with their beauty, attitude, and drama, but a male usually develops the situation into better things. Strengthen your weaknesses and keep them private. A weakness is not a weakness until it can be attacked. My first-time playing chess must've been beginners' luck, but I played this game with determination and confidence. I was feeling myself from the beginning of the game, and the person I was playing had plenty of experience. My opponent knew it was my first time playing, but what he didn't know was how badly I wanted to win.

It would amaze the world, how many individuals fear success to some degree. We have gatherings of individuals in America who endeavor to be successful but not rich. We have individuals who look down on individuals because they believe it's their fault that they're poor. I'm sure we've all heard about the people in life that are suffering mentally because they have lots of money. Obviously, this also means that there are people who are suffering because they do not have a lot of money. So, where do we genuinely find happiness?

We become happy when we become truly close with something or somebody we cherish. One of the reasons we discover it is so hard to discover happiness is because of our impression of what happiness truly is. Our capacity to be happy relies on how we characterize it.

There have been days in my life when I felt like I wasn't sure whether or not I was cheerful. For some, joy is characterized by what has been accomplished, what has been expertly completed, or material things we have attained. An extraordinary proposal to beginning your joy is knowing not to contrast yourself with others. Carrying on with our best life means concentrating on the feeling.

I think if we strive for happiness instead of success, then success will find us. Scot Spangler said, "Achievement is the point at which you can invest 90 percent of your energy doing the things you need to do and just 10 percent doing things you have to do.

Determination is a skill that can be learned! It requires setting objectives and being willing to buckle down, however it's very possible. Practice your certainty and flexible thinking in order to figure out how to view disappointments and obstacles as learning possibilities. The more we believe in ourselves, the better life will be. How can we accomplish a goal that we have already set doubt towards? Most importantly, we have told God that we do not believe in him to an extent. Because when you believe in Jesus, things will grab you easily. There is no failing when you are completely determined.

Confidence comes from loving yourself very much. I read in an article that people succeed in learning how to drive but fail at achieving other things. The answer to this conflict is straightforward: because we were certain that we could drive way before we sat in the driver's seat. You saw everybody around you succeeding in doing it, and you were convinced to that there's nothing very hard about it, despite the fact that it truly is a difficult assignment. Under the weight of this feedback, a few individuals question their own capacities and inevitably eventually give up. The few people who believe in themselves and who continue moving along the path they've chosen are the ones who succeed.

While speaking with two people, one day they were telling a kid that had not played football right after high school that he's not going to play football at UGA or no other big football school. The thing is, the two guys who were speaking were athletes that completely gave up on football because they wanted to make money doing other things that only last so long. So, the kid ran and told some wise people about his conversation with them. They told him that "the reason those guys made that comment was because they do not want to go through the hard work that it takes to make it to UGA so they're going to try to make you feel the same." How can a kid not make it wherever he wanted when all things are possible with God. Now the kid is determined to work harder than he ever had in his life because of those negative comments. A real friend wouldn't their friends dreamsif they're trying to do something that they love, no matter if they believe in them or not.

In almost every situation, where individuals give up on their objectives half-way through, they more often than not begin their assignment being totally persuaded with their thoughts, and are then put down by other individuals. Being put down is only being convinced that you are moving in the wrong direction. The issue with persuading individuals to have faith in something is that it should effectively be possible, no matter which option is correct! By any chance that you would prefer not to permit anybody to influence your choices or to put you down, find out about the brain science of persuading individuals. Persuading somebody to trust you is about persuading him to either acknowledge another conviction or upgrade his insight or convictions around a current thought. Not all individuals will acknowledge your thoughts from the first attempt, yet the uplifting news is that there are guidelines that can expand your chance of persuading other individuals to trust you.

In this lifetime, when people have failed at many things and are constantly being pushed back further, it's hard to watch someone who is steadily pushing forward. I told myself as a little boy that I can do two things in life; I can either get mad for watching people succeed or I can learn from them. I try my best to learn from everyone who is doing well and steady pushing forward in life. One day I woke up out my sleep determined to learn from other people.

Growing up, I would walk the streets of my old neighborhood and hear people talk about Steve Harvey's money, Oprah's money, T.I's money, Jay Z's money, etc. There was only one thing that frustrated me with this conversation, and it was the fact that I hadn't seen anyone putting in half the work doing the things those guys did to make the money. I would say "guys do you know that can be anybody? You, him, or me." They would say, "yes, man we're going to make it to the top one day" but wouldn't do anything to make it to the top. In fact, some things people do to make it to the top, like selling drugs, don't always pan out the way they might have hoped. An old man once told me those guys continue to say I'm going to stop when I reach a certain amount of money but it's only going to make them go harder to sell drugs because my generation would say the same thing and they all failed.

Possibly you purchase your drugs from a fine, upstanding native who simply happens to have a steady employment and a solid home life. There are sure administrations and frameworks which should be secured for the benefit of all. Those incorporate things like money, sustenance, prescription, pharmaceuticals, wellbeing and transportation. That is the reason the government offices exist, to keep up the quality and notoriety of these fundamental personal satisfaction issues. It isn't so much that it's fundamentally "wrong" to offer illegal drugs; it's simply not very wise.

Let's just say you get caught offering illegal drugs or unlawful medications, then you're screwed. If dope was legal, individuals would offer it and it would be exhausted leaving no one would believe it's the wrong thing to do. Since it is unlawful, individuals are going to consequently believe it's awful. It is not the general population that offers the medications that are in charge of the destroying of other individuals' lives. If those individuals choose to do medications and mischief, destroying their own particular physical and emotional well-being, that is on them. Consider the brief timeframe in our history where the administration prohibited liquor. It was most likely fundamentally the same to how pot is today. It was unlawful, however there were certainly individuals drinking it and offering it and they were most likely individuals who trusted that it wasn't right because it was illegal.

One thing about the black generation is I see people wanting to change but are stuck in an environment that they haven't been outside of, which makes it difficult to dream about a car you never saw or places you've never been. I know many people that have a college degree, but are struggling trying to pay back their student loans or find a job. Most Black kids struggle financially while attending college while White kids are getting allowances. Many White families start a college bank account for their kids while they're very young and it builds up yearly.

Anyhow, where I come from, it's hard to put money in a bank account when your parents already owe companies and different people. Black middle class income families still struggle despite having great and steady incomes. White students start their careers already ahead because they have a much lower loan burden than their Black counterparts. Black families are less likely to save and invest, resulting in less money for retirement and an inability to cope with major life events and emergencies that require money. In the end, Black families remain financially unstable and unable to accumulate wealth, while their White counterparts gain financial stability and build wealth.

Black women outnumber Black men in college enrollment, which shows that we have a desire to gain the skills and knowledge to lift ourselves out of poverty, but the student loans that accompany, dilute those efforts in getting an education. Mounting student debt is then often compounded by trying to survive in a single parent home where only one adult is responsible for bringing in an income and also trying to raise great kids. I try to build confidence in others by leading by example. People think what they say matters more than what they do. The best way for the Black community to improve is to come together.

I have dozens of White friends that I admire and follow behind because I see them doing things my own people are not doing. They teach me how to carry myself professionally, and how to become financially stable without selling drugs. I gain my confidence by surrounding myself with individuals who push themselves daily. People watch what you do more than they listen to what you say. Be someone worth emulating. My whole life I grew up around people who knew so much about reaching my dream, but as I grew older, I took the lead because they were doing more talking than anything. Look for people, ideas, environments, and knowledge that you find inspiring and motivating. I love to share my experiences because I believe it makes a difference in someone's life. When I share my failures and my successes, people find confidence in them.

8

DECISION MAKING

I think of the world as a gigantic grocery store. There are so many portions and possibilities. The endless combinations of ingredients one can purchase, the endless recipes that could be created, and the countless meals that can be made are just like the endless opportunities this world has for us. I wonder if I would be able to think of the same recipe sample as a friend of mine utilizing different ingredients. A sample is a little parcel of something to show what the whole is like. Since it's not very much, perhaps I could locate the ideal fixings just to make it taste somewhat similar. Individuals, for the most part, attempt to take the same course as others to get to the same destination. The fixings and formulas they utilize may not be for their wellbeing despite the destination. Feed yourself on what's beneficial for you and it might send you to a different course. God may need us to site see on our way to achievement. There are things we have to go over that will give us better thoughts. A few medications hurt others significantly more than they hurt us. Life can be precarious when we place our eye on other people's assignments. A task is something that is allocated for a person to abide with. All assignments aren't relegated for us. Sustain your body with the best possible advantages that will shine and become noticeable.

We often think that maybe if I go to college, I'll get a degree and live a happy life. Honestly, if you're not trying to be the best in the field you're interested in, you'll continue to give up on your potential. There are more competitors than we could ever imagine. We all have a dream. School isn't for everyone, neither is the military. Many of us go to college or the military to gain success. At whatever point we graduate high-school and don't have any arrangements in picking between the two, individuals naturally misjudge us. However, the most successful individuals on the planet never did not one or the other. In all actuality going to school or the military is never a poor decision. Dr. Seuss mentioned, "you have brains in your head, you have feet in your shoes, you can steer yourself any direction you choose."

A great way to start any day is to be brave and take positive risk: nothing can substitute experience. Julius

Caesar mentioned, "Experience is the teacher of all things." Sometimes we have to go through things rather than hear about them. Surviving certain risks can become the biggest fortunes of our lives. A mind that is stretched by a new experience can never go back to its old dimensions. Chances are odd of having the same aspects towards that situation. I love using quotes in conversations because it saves my peers from excuses. Excuses will always be here for us, but opportunities will not. Opportunities come within our chances of being successful. If my generation can find ways of being successful as much as we see each other's flaws, we'll be much farther ahead.

Numerous individuals that carry on with an inventive life are great at playing the hand they were dealt. People with less subsidizes are more creative naturally than people with more supports. Our family and friends are more likely to be creative, when their chances are limited. While our circumstances might make a specific compartment for our lives, it is our decisions that eventually decide how our lives will play out. A person who is not legitimately prepared to answer life's issues might turn from making progress, toward prevalence in valuable routes over that of an individual predominance at all expense. A hefty portion of our decisions originate from what we really have faith in. What will that fellow battle for? What does he talk about?

An inspired man will go to battle for his name before anything. How are these brave men standing up for their names, and under what conditions? Firstly, everything begins with certainty. For the general people who disagree, how about we simply say confidence is something that will weigh enormously on a scale. I went to a meeting at a Best Western hotel, Atlanta airport. I introduced myself genuinely, however, my confidence was the reason I didn't get hired. The manager asked me, "Why do you think we ought to hire you?" I reacted, "I think you guys ought to hire me since I think I have an awesome sense of humor, I'm extremely friendly, and so on." The words I and think together, kept me down. The awful thing is this was my second meeting at this Inn, and my fourth meeting where I didn't turn out with a job. Then again, I didn't tell myself those guys most likely didn't employ me because it was something about me, they just don't like or because I'm youthful or, inexperienced.

After we fall flat, we need to acknowledge life is too short to be stuck on the fizzling part. At some point, feeling frustrated about ourselves turns into an emotional habit that we convey into adulthood, where it turns into taking a risk in testing our circumstances, and the crazy ride of emotions that accompanies with it. The things I see and experience daily, remind me that everything occurs for a reason. The thing that pops up in my head in troublesome circumstances, is my ability to not compare my life with others. You may have noticed that every time we are facing a difficult session in our life, there are always people who would say "everything is going to be okay", "things are going to get better", "better days are coming", and more.

For the most part life is a circle and so is the globe. Life situations go around in a circle, which make these things go around and come around. These things distract us from the positive route in life and even our purposes. Many of us are searching for our "life purpose." I'm not sure that that's something we can easily uncover. In my experience, it unfolds over a lifetime. But what we can do, is create meaning for our lives. We can take the hand we're dealt and ask, how can we make the most of what we've been given? How can I be a better person? How can I contribute to myself, those close to me, and the world? How can I find the courage to pursue what I'm passionate about? When I focus on questions like that, the fact that I wasn't born rich or beautiful, or that I can't draw, or that my parents never encouraged me to get a PhD, just doesn't matter. In fact, a lot of things don't matter but the ingredients we feed ourselves daily. I met a friend at Morehouse University who said to me, his biggest frustration in life was that he hadn't accepted himself for who he was. The conversation continued and I asked him what he thinks he needs to do about it. He said he wanted to change. My response to him was how are you going to change when you haven't even accepted yourself.

Sometimes we imagine we should be something other than what we are. Maybe I wasn't made to leave one of the biggest legacies in history. These thoughts hold millions of people back from great opportunities every day. We all have a gift that will impress the world. God's gifts are the greatest gifts we could ever accept. In order to achieve your maximum potential, first you need to discover a position of complete acknowledgment of who you are. Life is not about contrasting, judging, or changing who we are to fit in. Life is not about attempting to step as others to achieve achievement or looking down on ourselves around individuals that are doing better than us. When we find ourselves and love ourselves, we open ourselves up to additional things.

The thing is nobody needs to live for years and years then acknowledge they've been keeping themselves away from awesome things in view of inability to accept themselves. We accept who we are at the point when we aren't attempting to change who we are. One thing is for sure, we need to give up the thought that we might be something that we aren't. Take a gander at yourself as the individual you are, and carry on with that individual life, minus all potential limitations. Try not to take a gander at yourself from a position of what you envision others may think.

Others will not hand you achievement, bliss, or affection.

The way people are nowadays, individuals are envious and barbarous. There are too many people that are satisfied with a person not accepting themselves and that is enough happiness for them. The best stride to seeing who you truly are is to trust that you are what you are. When you have confidence in which you will be, you will be all right. When you acknowledge yourself dependably, you will never feel less than, or unworthy, or without certainty. Acknowledgment assumes the greatest part in our self-esteem. By tolerating yourself totally, you are relinquishing the thought that you are insufficient. The greater part of this is that you are to be. Acknowledge yourself and wake up to the genuine you.

I read a joke on a site about a man that had strolled into a doctor's office with a cucumber in his nose, a carrot in one ear, and a banana in the other ear. He spoke to the doctor about not receiving the proper nourishment. The doctor told the gentleman, obviously you're not.

The purpose of the joke is how he wasn't feeding himself appropriately. A fellow that smokes on a daily will more likely become exhausted quicker than a man who doesn't smoke. Many days of my life, I bounce on the treadmill or run a couple of laps to improve myself. My issues don't blur away, yet I'm not as worried about my issues as I was before. This gives me a point of view with less weight on my shoulders. I dream about heading off to the rainforest, jungle, or a wilderness to watch the waterfalls. A man would see how inventive they can be when they learn more about themselves daily.

I wrote a poem in class at Georgia Perimeter College. The poem was based on a true story. My poems help me escape my mind prison.

My poem went like this:

While sleeping and dreaming, I discovered a compass.
   all of a sudden I was woken by a rumpus,
   I finished my dream by using my gift,
the compass was all a blessing that caused all my enemies to shift.

The fantasy depended on me listening to pessimistic individuals and taking in some of their ways and words. In my dream, I was headed to hang out with some guys to find ways to make money. The guys had messaged me their current location, so I put the address in my GPS. The address I typed into my phone sent me to a weird location that delayed me and put me behind time. I called the guys repeatedly over and over, but no one answered. Then I turned back around and went home. The guys ended up contacting me hours later, apologizing about not answering their phone.

The thing is, I discovered the guys on their

SnapChat with females. I thought to myself, is this the reason these guys didn't answer after I drove thirty minutes and sat in traffic an additional twenty minutes? The very next day, those guys wanted to meet up halfway, and I went to the location they messaged me. I sat in the car looking for them for a pretty decent time and they never showed up. Days later, they apologized again. The very next week these guys called me asking to meet up. I told them, "no, I'm cool. You guys can go ahead without me." The same day, those three guys ended up getting killed at the location we were supposed to meet. While all this was going on, I didn't feel like these guys had my best interest in mind. The dream felt so real, I woke up out of my sleep.

Bad things sometimes have to happen in order for us to shift in another lane. In case you're afraid to accomplish something, maybe that is the very thing you ought to do. When you have to deal with discomfort or a fearful circumstance, you turn out on the other side better prepared to handle fear the next time you confront it.

I'm the type of guy that will volunteer doing something positive that I fear because I'm in love with benefiting myself that much. Whenever I want someone to read something that I've written or want someone to help me with a situation, I'll go to a complete stranger.

This way, feeling isn't involved and I would sink into the truth much faster. We as people, should attempt to understand things we love or things that have the potential to work in our favor.

The more we feel comfortable being alone, the more we will be inspired to improve ourselves and decisions. Searching for ways to improve our potential should become a habit and something we are in love with.

9

THE WAY TO ACHIEVEMENT

The way to achievement is playing the hand you were dealt. Maybe you were appointed to the wrong group of individuals.

What's a good idea for you to pursue? In a card game, you would adjust the cards to win. The hand that is dealt to you can come down to determination; the way you play it is free will. Leave negative individuals and terrible circumstances.

What other hand are you going to play? Some get dealt a great hand. Others take an average or even poor hand and work it into a winner. Still others will squander a great hand.

Here and there, we need to surround ourselves with better circumstances and intellectual people. Every decision we make, we ought to place ourselves in the wisest circumstance. Our thinking becomes our habits, which becomes our natural reflexes.

Anyone familiar with cards knows, the luck is in the cards; the skill is in the player. Learning the game is part of playing well. But you only have the cards you have. Sometimes you just have to work through this hand and hope the next hand is better. But you must do what you can with what you have.

You never want to get too comfortable with making mistakes. Salvador Dali said, "Intelligence without ambition is a bird without wings."

You can get better by practicing. You can get better by observing what good players do or don't do, and in what circumstances. You can get better by reading books by good players. You can get better by understanding the odds and probabilities of the game. You can get better by practicing more.

Love your knowledge and use it to the best of your advantage. Make every move like it's the last opportunity to become successful. When you notice that every decision was your best decision, you trust yourself more and love your trust. Cherishing yourself feeds your body with nutrients. At the point when something doesn't challenge you, it won't change you. No one wants to go through tough obstacles. The way to achievement does not differ from preparing for a sports game all week long to win the victory at the end of the week. Those obstacles make us a better player for the next game and the next trial in life.

Many individuals choose school or the military to

reach success. These things are never a bad decision. You need explicit knowledge or courage to become successful without an education. A man can turn into a very successful person by sitting at a computer throughout the day regardless of what position he's in. There are many individuals without a definite purpose. The bigger the hole we are in, the better and quicker we have to think. When you're definite about something, you're fully committed. Most of your days will be planned around your definite purpose. A degree is a piece of paper that will give us advantages in that field.

A degree and a profession fall into the same class. The things we learn are not always the things we love or admire. We are experts at our talent and the things we love. Whenever we learn something that we love, we become great at it. You can't teach talent. A person usually loves things they're half-way decent at. A job is a place that will occupy us as the days progress. However, a few jobs are exceptionally charming with regards to fulfilling a dream.

It is a great decision to progress your talent to reach success. Our talent would be something we love to pursue daily. A gift is something that we fall asleep just to wake up for. Maybe we choose to make do with an occupation or a profession there will be room to get better at.

As I became saved, I understood regardless of how much I've progressed, there will always be space for improvements. Kim Collins said, "Strive for continuous improvement, instead of perfection."

Let's not be fulfilled, but keep on progressing. Sometimes we tumble off the wrong track and never advance back. Many individuals experience things that give them a negative point of view. When we are around adverse individuals, we feel dimness over us. An intelligent man once said to me, "We typically see things before they happen."

God, in some cases, furnishes us with looks without bounds. We don't need to investigate the future to look for illustrations of the anger of man because it has been working on earth since Cain and Able.

God permits awful things to transpire, however, he doesn't bring about them. He cautions us that he cherishes us; actually, he guaranteed he would help us through it. God doesn't keep these things from happening because he has reasons of not interceding and not mediating in an individual's lives. Individuals misunderstand that God's ways are not our ways and his contemplations are not our musings. We are here to skate through the pleasures of life but avoid any thin ice.

Before we make it to thin ice, our conscience warns us about the violation of a moral law. Our small voice will just help us on the off chance that it has been protected or prepared, and it must be educated by reality and prepared like a muscle. We should talk about enhancing individuals and be people of motivation.

In the first place, we need to recognize the reality individuals watch what we accomplish more than they listen to what we say. Individuals couldn't care less about the amount you know until they discover the amount you give. I love connecting emotionally with people by listening to what they have to say. In order to get someone to listen to you, first you have to notify them that they are very important. We should complement our peers daily. A compliment a day is a superior path forward.

Certainty is a little thing that will definitely expand our perseverance. Enhancing a man will enhance their associates. We all merit a magnificent future. Life is pointless without a future. What's to come is the best thing about existence.

Our desire is to win over our rival and separate us from the normal. Desire is a force which impacts more than our profession. I learned during a gathering meeting that aspiration is a standout amongst the most vital devices to make progress. Being capable is pointless without the desire to bolster it.

Too much ambition makes people view us as cocky or conceited. Sometimes we have to introduce people to make their minds visualize better. Knowledge is the backbone of society's progress. However, the average adult only uses 10% of their brain. Distractions are sometimes those thoughts that interact in our mind without permission. Life will take you down roads that make us conscious of our own consciousness. Observing our thoughts is one of the creative tools for better ambition. We have to separate our thoughts like words on a paper; it can sometimes make a mess and become very annoying.

I once heard a man ask a lady, "How is life." She replied, "I can't complain," and he replied, "It wouldn't help no way."

This was one of the most inspirational choices of words I've ever witnessed. The issue I find in today's public is not how our era doesn't know how to think, it's that we don't think. I've met individuals who think before they respond, yet they have to change the way they think before they respond. We can turn into the master of our space. At the point when speculation is out of request and indistinct, our reasoning gets to be out of request and hazy. At whatever point we choose to add new learning, we need to enhance the procedure of including new information.

In order to avoid certain obstacles, first we have to be aware of our potential biases. We have to compare and contrast our thoughts to the objective learning style. The issue I find in today's public is not how our generation doesn't know how to think, but that we don't think too much about anything.

I have personal meetings with myself because I'm so eager to succeed and help others succeed. My personal board meetings are things I should improve and things

I need to add to my notepad. I break down my yearly goals into monthly goals so my task will be simple to execute. The only hard thing about completing my task is getting started.

Without a start, there will never be a finish and that's why I never understand why people postpone things. A considerable lot of us are involved with the achievement of others.

Growing up as a child, I saw cars that were dope and my friends would go insane. My companions would even discuss how that individual was so affluent and in the back of my mind, I said, *some person invest the push to buy those sort things.*

After a few days, I end up agonizing over an excess of things to help my prosperity. I recognized the most ideal approach to fulfill an inquisitive personality is to let in awe. Most things move with our assistance, and a few things require significant investment. There will dependably be a battle towards dealing with our desire.

10

MONEY TRAIN

Life is a business. Many of us wonder why marijuana isn't legal in more prominent areas of the states of America. As far as anyone is concerned, the government can't tax it, which means it doesn't benefit them financially. Individuals have said this medication has to be illicit, including an experimental produce. In 1619, the state of Virginia chose they were going to develop this plant on homesteads. Drug stores in many countries were putting this medication to use. This medication is seen as addictive while tobacco items are just as addictive, but were placed in stores before marijuana was legal.

Correspondents have acknowledged that this medication has high potential for misuse. Weed can help many aliments, taking into account glaucoma, growth, diabetes, and so on. One of the issues with legalizing this medication is the way that it has been described as a terrible medication for individuals.

Business is about profit. I remember when I was eight years old going to a primary school in Orlando, Florida when my educator said to me, "Vew math as an instrument." Most individuals I've been around think math is difficult to learn. At whatever time we view something as troublesome, we more often than not, don't set aside a few minutes to better ourselves at these things. Math is a type of imagination.

Many individuals smoke pot to support their inventiveness and perspectives from an alternate point of view. This medication turns in to a vast impact on people's state of mind that unwinds the brain. However, breathing in smoke is a terrible for a variety of reasons.

Cannabis will give a great deal of organizations loads of cash. Business is about money. Math has constantly been one of my most adored subjects. I understand the attributes of math uncommonly well. Functions are one of the few math correlations that are dependable and significant in this reality.

Formulas and inclinations make out bits of knowledge on an outline and if the spots are all over the place, your graph and your business are pointless. When all the dots are combined and congested together, this is a way to decide how many pounds should a 12-year-old weigh at a certain height, or how fast a car is traveling when wrecks occur on a curve.

For instance, "Street slopes are intended to run water off the street or in a channel to maintain a strategic distance from puddles." In building streets, one must figure out how the slope of the street will be. Snowboarders and skiers must know about risk zones. While developing wheelchair inclines a slant is critical. Math that children learn toward the start of evolution in school is the establishment of the work they're going to do past that.

The vast majority say that math isn't essential because of the challenges that accompany it. People will speak antagonistically about math around their youngsters; that places them in a shocking viewpoint towards the vibe of math. Kids grow up saying we do math that we don't even need in this present reality. When people talk pessimistically about a subject around young individuals, their kids grow up not as open to learn much about the subject. An environment has an interwoven attachment to learning. Math is what we make it, it can be absolutely fun.

The subject of science is essential for building a kid's potential. An extensive amount of things we learn in math, we apply in unmistakable ways later. One thing I despised about school was the way that teachers will markdown wrong answers on our papers.

Every now and again, a wrong answer is wrong, not because the student didn't know the answer, but because many kids freeze up in testing situations. I don't think school tests ought to be an extreme objective. Genuine objectives of instruction ought to be that the students are readied to do math in this present reality. At the point when individuals fear committing errors, they're very anxious about discovering something new, inventive, or thinking differently.

Our mind develops and creates new associations while mistakes are being made. Timed tests sends the mind a message that math is about execution, which is extremely deceptive. We need to comprehend things and their relationship towards one another.

All organizations are about insights. Business arithmetic is used by business undertakings to record and oversee operations. I met a fellow in Miami, Florida that said, "Marijuana will close down many organizations in America in the event it is legalized."

I perceived later that may be the reason cannabis hasn't been legalized. Regulating the financial liabilities in your business is the way to achievement, which is important towards beneficial operations.

11

MOTIVATION

My motivation in life is to follow in the Lord's footsteps. When we follow someone who's already been to the place we're trying to go, they can never mislead us. The older we get in life, the more we expect.

The greatest difference between college and grad school is what professors expect from the students. Grad school classes develop a sense of knowledge, while college professors prefer their students analyze their learning. The older we become, individuals should have the capacity to furnish our data with evidence.

Analyzing refers to critical thinking. The best speakers are extraordinary analyzers in addition to speaking actualities, yet they can furnish you with as much data as you need. We don't only want to hear facts, but we want you to explain why it's true.

Discussions without points of interest are sometimes useless. An awesome communicator can win in various ways because it's not about what you say, but how you say it. In school, while composing an article, it's not about what you compose, but how you compose it.

Northerners are generally better writers then southerners because their English is more professional. Northerners typically speak as if they were writing. Their discussions are more energetic, which prompts to bigger morals. At the point when morals fall in place, business falls next. This refers to higher levels of conversation, which proceeds into complex ideas.

12

JUDGING

America is an exceedingly judgmental nation by our use of words and our activities. As a nation, when we lay our eyes upon individuals who are dressed improperly or one that is using foul language, we choose to look down on them. While being an offspring of God, I recognize that a judge doesn't have any privilege to look down on a criminal. A millionaire doesn't have any right to look down on a poor person. A judge doesn't have any privilege to misjudge individuals that God is satisfied with. The treatment and emotions the criminals receive by guards in jail are harmful.

God anticipates that we will judge others. We live in a society where individuals are going to judge, however not all of them are doing it deliberately. I would rather a person hate me for who I am, than love me for who I'm not.

To a degree, we all care about what people think of us. We want others to see us in a specific light. Sometimes others hate us for who they want us to be. Worrying about what others think can interfere with our own instinct. There is a wide range of recipes of judgment.

Judging between which quarterback will begin this year is a splendid thought. Nobody needs to have an unsuccessful season. Everything football players experience is sufficiently tough. In life, we are permitted to judge once we've found ourselves. I asked myself would I have the capacity to be blundering against God in case I declined to judge my love ones.

How might we be able to detect terrible things and love great things in the event that we aren't already judging? In my personal journey of trying to become a better person, I realized it's all about aiming to be happy. One of the things I strive to do is to keep toxic people from dumping their poison onto me.

The right judgment is never a frightful thing for our partners and a delight to God. Everyone has things that are hard to control. In any case we're not expected to contribute most of our vitality judging. We're depended upon to judge through the book of scriptures. We shouldn't pass judgment on things God doesn't identify with.

Individuals can be so built up to judge a man and bring up all their imperfections when it isn't their place to do such. Things aren't terrible or great if they're not controlled by God's statement.

Our beliefs are judging tools we shouldn't use often. Conclusions are sometimes things that don't always make a difference. Opinions can be based upon wrong certainties or an off-base application. A terrible application could demolish a person's purpose or do significantly worse. Our attitudes toward things could be better by speaking empowering words from the heart.

Here and there, the smallest words can make a person's day. I discovered that it turns into a characteristic device to question a man. Questioning a man while seeking the best afterwards doesn't identify with a judgment of sin.

Perhaps a companion of our own conceives that they have an awesome shot of being a pioneer at this new organization downtown. While questioning a companion and letting them know you have confidence in them will help them succeeded.

At the point when a child is told at an early age that they're skilled and charming, they grow up trusting it for eternity! Individuals have a tendency to accept what they hear many times. Our own particular impressions are affected by what we see to be the truth of others.

For instance, a congressman may get many telephone calls from a few constituents asking for a an approach to be embedded or changed. From those solicitations, he must choose how voters in their state feel about the issue.

A hefty portion of us just listen to the data that we want to hear rather than what we need to hear. People avoid information that contradicts what they already think or believe. Individuals have a tendency to maintain a strategic distance from data that negates what they think or accept. Sometimes we question for the wrong reasons.

We have a tendency to despise our companion's ability on the grounds that we are hesitant to see them surpass us. Every once in a while, our associates appear to know things we don't understand, which may decide who achieves a sure objective the quickest.

At last, our associates can be our endowments. Each minute we spend on higher awareness inspires the cognizance of the world. The better our considerations, the better our results. Our contemplations will dependably decide our day. Many things we relate to do can be stayed away from by our musings. Contentions and open deliberations can be controlled by the way we handle them.

God's words can never be a contention or levelheaded discussion. These are types of mankind. We can't scrutinize God's decision of words in light of the fact that he's ideal in all ways.

When a man looks for God, they discover peace. God will show his kin how to judge profoundly.

A molded brain loves and despises the correct

things. Having faith in things that aren't true can have us frequently caught in anguish. Judgments make a separation in the middle of individuals and what they're judging.

Peace makes us feel bald faced and extremely positive about our reasoning. I want to criticize against things that don't accompany peace. At the point when our psyche is not caught into the negative world, positive things appear to discover us.

While chatting with a companion one day, he recognized how individuals control the rhythm of their day to day lives. Controlling the rhythm identifies with adjusting an item. While adjusting an item, this shows the psyche that we are in control of the rhythm. For example, while living in a few nations, you may recognize the thinking of why there are speed limits. Driving too fast or too slow can prompt death.

In this present reality, moving too fast or too moderate in choice making can prompt tragedies. You and a circumstance are joined as one, which prompts you into telling the brain that there is capacity. At the point when the psyche finds capacity, it has confidence in its potential. We get to be mindful of our brain action.

While growing up, I recognized that individuals aren't going to have the same understanding as me. You can't be genuine with fake individuals in this present reality. I had a discussion with a companion of mine. He inferred to me that the street I'm on isn't intended for everybody to travel. I catch myself trying to hold on to people that God is telling me to let go of. I look for my potential better when I'm around individuals who have confidence in the same dreams I do.

Potential is an instrument we can use every day. The most noteworthy purpose of our potential is found through our certainty mode. I discovered that the human personality can't understand the way of an entire universe. Thoughts on why things work the way they do may be unanswered until the end of time. We can find out why things happen the way they do.

Potential is being judged by our companions each day. Picking not to judge will place you in a fellowship with life itself. Individuals that put stock in themselves the most are typically the general population. We have an extremely solid personality in regard to controlling a win-or-lose circumstance. God gave us the capacity to lead ourselves in the right heading. I've met individuals who knew that they discovered peace while discovering achievement.

One of the best safe places ever is achievement. Achievement isn't about monetary principles and obligation. Achievement can be found through appreciation. The vast majority views accomplishment by the measure of cash. There are many lower-class nationals who are fulfilled by their lives. At the point when a man is observed to be fulfilled by their life, they've discovered achievement.

We all have kindred companions or partners that survive paycheck to paycheck. The main individuals we find to be unsatisfied are the ones who aren't fulfilled by their outcomes. Results are a kind of thankfulness letter or a letter of inspiration capacity.

It is extremely unlikely that we were destined to pay bills and kick the bucket. Now and then God can favor us by bringing down our regularly scheduled installments. I'll gain the satisfaction of achievement speedier than a man who has kept the same number of assets by the way that my credit is vastly improved.

Here and there, life can appear to be so spoiled. Regardless of how hard we try, it appears like we end up in deadlocks. We can't dispatch our awesome arrangements and fundamental systems. We look down on ourselves on the grounds that it appears that everybody around us is living happily ever after. I've ended up in numerous battles thinking, what are they doing another way.

Why is it such a battle for me?

Life appears to have arbitrary occasions that constantly fall in our direction. Many things appear to meddle with our day-to-day assignments. For example, a passing in the family, being let go from our employment, an ailment, and so on.

A great deal of times things happen because of our terrible decision making. We persistently work in the same way, taking after the same example and taking a shot at the same riddle. These things are negative behavior patterns that are difficult to break.

I think every once in a while, individuals overlook the fact that we have the ability to succeed with whatever we're conceived with. Ordinarily, a man will locate an alternate way when they've understood they can't proceed the old way anymore. A judge may at present believe you're liable after you have showed honesty. Once in a while, individuals lounge around and discuss things and individuals in light of the fact that they don't have anything else to discuss.

Here and there, life hit us with an incredible update that moves our point of view. There have been times throughout my life where anything that could turn out badly did just that. God has reminded me things need to turn out badly before they can go right. Open doors are found in the season of extraordinary trouble. You will confront the best resistance when you are nearest to your greatest supernatural occurrence. Permit yourself to develop and change.

The main thing you must be is uncertain. Change is excruciating. I discovered that nothing is more difficult than staying stuck where you don't have a place. While eating with one of my kindred fellow team members, he informed me, "It's better to endeavor to do impeccable and fall flat, than to endeavor to do nothing and succeed."

The joy of our life relies on the nature of our considerations. Our considerations can be worth a great amount of money when worked the right way, because you are what you think. By what means would we be able to change something without changing our reasoning?

A splendid day will start with a brilliant mentality. We need to consider life a gift, keeping in mind the end goal is to experience it that way. A genuine individual will shake the world and the general population around gently.

Ordinarily, I've overlooked my needs and wound up in gaps that are hard to leave. We meet no standard things or individuals throughout our life. Everything around us fills a need. Once in a while, my reasoning can make me feel like one of the most bizarre individuals on the planet. And in that same instance, I think a number of individuals feel the same.

The hardest thing to do in intense circumstances is to change our psyche from a negative thought to a positive thought. As I became more established, I understood that I didn't have the privilege to judge individuals through my assessment.

Truth be told, I reminded myself to not stress over my battles and take baby steps in life. Life is basic, yet it requires exertion. My otherworldly side has demonstrated to me a superior path forward and how to judge.

13

EXISTENCES

A standout among the most wonderful things about existence, is being compensated for what you've worked for. Every now and again, regardless of how hard we work, a few individuals will be unsatisfied with our effort. Bosses will fire you and educators and people will censure your efforts. Speaking with a gentleman in downtown Atlanta one day, he informed to me that "on the off chance that you know you're accomplishing something right and nobody else concurs, overlook it." Life is the viewpoint of things. Each circumstance has an incredible method for reacting to it. While living through tragedies, the most noticeably awful thing to do is to thump yourself about it.

We as individuals love to be entertained in some type of way. For sure, we all pine for respect beyond any doubt. We are social animals, yet a couple of us go an extra mile to perform something, paying little mind to the great or terrible. For instance, various people live past their budgetary points of interest considering how people buy things they can hardly manage. Many times, our youth encounter influencers in their adulthood.

Individuals who had little lee way were brought up in a way that makes them search for consideration. These individuals discover this as a way of saving their mental equalization. A child will dependably attempt and copy the good conditions they experienced in childhood. At whatever point a man is talking from a motivational standpoint, or on a subject of essentials to an assemblage, there will dependably be that individual that is cheerful enough to yell their considerations so everyone can hear. These sorts of things are insane to me because I've never comprehended the motivation behind why individuals do it, particularly when somebody is speaking about the same point.

At whatever point a companion or an associate is more effective in the same vocation or working environment, we prefer not to hear these individuals speak of their advantages. We attempt to conceal our desire by saying the things we're great at. At whatever point somebody is fulfilled by their outcomes, they truly don't hint at any envy. We abstain from talking about things we're normally effectively fulfilled by. We add to our drives and impulses based upon the things we encounter. Many things get to be nature reflexes for whatever remains of our lives. At whatever point you're expanding on a circumstance, and nobody is supplementing or censuring your work, you might work harder or surrender.

Our mind is the most intense instrument we are honored with. A part of being developed is having information on life itself. When we figure out how to manage contrary individuals and negative circumstances, we've discovered development. Now and then we must choose the option to manage adverse individuals, yet it's about how we manage these individuals that characterize us. At whatever point we discover tolerance, we discover placidness and unwinding. While being quiet, we change the way we see diverse circumstances. I discovered that staying positive is the expert approach to act towards antagonistic circumstances.

Sometmes our negative responses aggravate circumstances and we wind up baffled or outraged. The mentality we bring to a negative circumstance is a decision. In the business world, keeping an uplifting disposition in negative circumstances is a significant aptitude to learn. These things take disciplinary work to fulfill. However, when I don't succeed at things that I'm working towards, I think of it as a preparation program. I've heard individuals say not to react out of feeling. Figure out how to manage anxiety to evacuate antagonism. Albert Einstein said, "Amidst trouble lies opportunity." As humans, we shouldn't permit our supposition of somebody to end up bored by a negative circumstance. Be proactive rather than receptive when managing unfavorable circumstances. A negative response to things outside our control is a waste of time. We shouldn't let the angle, qualities, or thinking, swing us to the dim side of our workforce.

14

EMOTIONS

Emotions rule the world in many formulas. Confusion, sadness, happiness, and anger sometimes impede things. There aren't many things that can impede the things we truly love. Priorities are things we ought to love the most because when they're in order, our life falls in order. While priorities are being taken care of properly, other things fall into place promptly. The best thing about tomorrow is that it's an opportunity to be a better you. I love to wake up thinking about at least one positive thing I would love to explore. This way, no matter what the rest of my day comprises, I know I did something to better myself. Days are usually passing us by and we're steadily planning for the next day. Sticking with this mindset is usually one reason why people don't make it as far as they could've. People sometimes forget that you have to be greater than most of the world to be ahead. We have to outwork the people we see every day to land on top or ahead.

Everyone has been blessed with a gift that is worth a million dollars or more, but it's all about what you do with what you have. Using your gift to its full potential can turn into the best feeling in the world. Using our gift to its full potential gives us the feeling of winning the lottery, or finding a fortune, one of those moods we can't describe in words. Being broke today and waking up rich tomorrow is very possible. In fact, things happen overnight the more we believe in Jesus. The things we believe in will always be nearest to us, even family and friends. Whenever we have genuine love for a person, they tend to feel the connection. For example, in order to feed certain animals, you often must set their food away from you in order to get them to eat it. The more you feed these animals, the more you will begin to bring the food closer to you. The animal will eventually start to feel more comfortable with your presence, and will come closer to you.

One of the best ways to make people interested in you is to make them feel important. People love to feel like they matter, which helps to take away any insecurities they may have. There are thousands of simple ways to make our peers feel important. Many times, when we see an old friend at the grocery store, we rarely go into much detail in the conversation. Maybe the person mentioned an event they were going to attend. The next time we see them it doesn't hurt to ask how the event went, no matter if we do not see them until months later. I usually seek to find out a lot about a person throughout our first conversation. Many people I meet love to be complimented in front of others. Humans love to be asked certain questions like "what is your favorite song?" However, when a person begins a conversation and is interrupted, be the first to tell them to continue with the story. Our peers and loved ones will react differently when we put time into their world, encouraging them. After meeting someone new, it doesn't hurt to check up on them through an email or sticky note.

When we show love, it returns. Recognize what is special about the people in your circle that you're dealing with; encounter their everyday decisions with your best choice of words. We as people fall flat on our shoulders when we begin to expect things in return. We enjoy being complimented and bragged about, so we should enjoy complimenting and bragging about others as much as necessary. In this world as we know, it's anything but difficult to concentrate on ourselves, our objectives, our wishes, and our arrangements. There's something motivating unique about any individual who makes it a need to genuinely see and recognize the general population around them. The sad thing is we usually miss the signs that are showing us to focus outside ourselves.

Life becomes fun when we put one foot in front of the other consistently. When someone is in our circle, our life gets better as their life becomes better. The strings that are attached to us are strings that are a part of our lives. String we are around the most will be the shortest strings. The shortest strings mean we are more a part of that person's life. What they do for themselves will reflect on you more than any other string. People that can more relate to specific things develop the better relationships.

The art of learning how to love and unite with others is priceless. Regardless of how long we may live, you'll never quit learning. Each moment brings new chances to learn something we've never known. For whatever length of time that we're interested in, God will keep on teaching us consistently. Despite everything I'm learning, and I know I will be. What God shows me consistently about affection keeps on changing my life. I've gone to where I can genuinely say, "Ruler, dispense with everything in my life that is keeping me down. If you don't mind, take away anything that is keeping me from strolling in affection and discovering genuine satisfaction in my life."

A standout among the most imperative aspects I've learned about affection is unselfishness, which is portrayed in the Bible as an eagerness to relinquish one's own desires for those of others. I've discovered that intimate romance will adjust and change in accordance with the requirements and desires of individuals. It's incomprehensible for individuals who've really been diminished to love, to be narrowminded. God has taught them how to be absolutely versatile and customizable to others. Selfish individuals, then again, have hard hearts. It's extremely troublesome for them to learn anything, particularly things that include selflessness. They anticipate that other people will conform to them and their needs. They essentially don't know how to change in accordance with others, without becoming sad or upset.

Figuring out how to adjust and change in accordance with the requirements and goals of others was exceptionally difficult for me. To be completely forthcoming, I wanted my way, and I got upset when I didn't get it. I was selfish! I wanted what I thought I needed, when I wanted it! I couldn't stand waiting on another person, or bowing my own particular wishes to suit another person's comfort. In any case, God started to mellow my heart, and slowly I figured out how to see the requirements of others. At that point, God gave me compassion and the genuine longing to address the issues of others first, before my own. Gradually, I became focused on strolling with affection. I figured out how to adjust my own particular needs and goals to address the issues of others. I figured out how to show love in various approaches to various individuals. Not all individuals need the same thing from us. One of our kids, for instance, may require more of our own time than the others. One of our companions may require more support all the time than another.

Love can be strange and terrific because of its ability to train others. As children or teenagers, we rarely understand or feel the real meaning of love. While conversing with my uncle one day, he said to me, "I didn't learn how to love until I had my first child." Sometimes God brings things to our attention when we run out of options. Growing up, it can be very easy and normal to love only the things that will benefit us in return. The longer we live with that mentality, the longer it will take us to understand the bigger areas in life. Younger people are good at confusing love with feelings. For most Westerners, their connections are the one aspect of our lives that we are glad to leave completely to risk. We arrange our instruction, our professions, our accounts, our retirement, yet we're still uncomfortable with arranging our peer's lives. However, for a long time, romantic affection was seen as a type of franticness, and energy wasn't viewed as an honest to goodness premise for marriage until late times.

So why do we place such an emphasis on emotions? The issue begins with children's stories. They encourage some exceptionally flexible myths. The myth that I am referring to is the idea of the 'one' is another exceptionally damaging error. We trust the one that is out there for us, as if no one but we can discover him or her. We think once we locate the One, he or she will never show signs of change, and neither will we. How do these myths influence us? They impact how we select a partner. On the chance that you think you cherish somebody immediately, you're enamored with a romanticized variant of the individual, or, similar to Shakespeare's Duke Orsino, you're just 'infatuated with adoration. The children's stories urge us to search for the lightning jolt. However, connections considering this sort of marvel, quite often end in batters. This sort of quick bond was seen as a sort of frenzy. Additionally, when our desires are disregarded, when our spouse cheats, puts on weight or quits lying down with us, we get discouraged or angry.

The things we love or have emotions for that have nothing for us in return can dislocate some of the positive segments within our thoughts. Emotions come in a thousand different shapes and sizes. The way we use emotions can change someone's life or even our own. The way we respond to emotions can carry us a long way. Emotions will always rule the world, friendships, relationships, and more. The only way America will become better is if we utilize our emotions.

15

FINDING YOURSELF

Between the ages of 18-22 people can be a very insecure. A major mind difficulty is going on because you're wondering what's next and if you're doing enough to make it through another obstacle. Your peers are discussing your future with their input and output on what they believe your future will gradually become. Families and friends begin to depend on you and expect big things, but you can very easily let them down with one mistake. You're sort of grown, but you're really not quite sure on how to be grown when dealing with responsibilities. Once we walk across the stage after high school, its like we're thrown in an ocean and someone says to swim on your own for eternity. We're being chastised by contradicting individuals that teach us to have a mind of our own. Sometimes a mind of our own is not accepted by individuals that disagree with the choices we make.

I'm sure we've all met individuals that disagree with choices that aren't wrong because it's not a part of their personality. It's quite difficult to please everyone, however, some people will judge you for not being the person they want you to be. Some people's reactions to certain situations may differ from our reaction. However, sometime it's not about what idea is the best, it's about what idea is the best for you. Society easily judges people that think differently and handle situations differently from them. When emotions are involved in situations, people begin to over think or not think enough. Have you ever heard anyone say, "I do not mix business with pleasure"? The brain works and handles the business through emotions. Things can break into pieces when more emotions are used than rational business decisions.

Growing up, I faced a hard time with believing in myself. I would think it was something about me that just wasn't big enough for the world. The times I was picked at and laughed at, gave me the work ethic that I have today. I became emotionally upset to the point where I found a desire to outwork the people that cracked jokes about me. The older I became, the better I responded to these situations, helping them to fade away. My power to remember any and every way someone has treated me is insane. Once I found myself, I realized even if I'm handed the opportunity to look down on the individuals who laughed at me, I refused to. In fact, I will help them if necessary because God's work will stick out for itself.

Most of my life I've had difficulty with dealing with people. My tolerance for individuals is very low because I can become irritated by someone's presence. Somehow, I outgrew things before many people my age. My thoughts towards life are traveling around the world doing things I love. My type of partying is taking my family to a wonderful city to enjoy the skyline and the culture of local food and music. I find myself dozing off, thinking about reality more often than normal. The thoughts I discover make me want to discuss them with the world. I'm usually discovering signals that are telling me a lot about a situation that I am experiencing, but my weirdness towards reality makes me respond awkwardly. I have to experience things that I'm already aware of in order for it to sink in. I'm still learning how to deal with my own perception of reality. My way of dealing with my perceptions is to write or discuss the topic with someone.

One of the most difficult experiences to deal with is wondering what your purpose in life is. If we're talented at something we love to do, we're automatically supposed to assume that's our purpose. The way you end up toward the end of a trip is if at your last destination there's a gigantic mirror that reflects to who you are as a person. Suddenly, the possibility of me searching for myself appeared to be insane. It resembles walking into a room brimming with individuals and not finding you among them. Clearly you won't wind up among the group, as you are the very thing that is doing the looking! It resembles how the eye can see everything except for itself. It's searching for your shades when they're on your face. You can look in all the intricate spots you want, yet you'll never discover them until you stop and look in a mirror. To find yourself, first you need to find out about yourself. Finding the genuine you is illuminating. You get to be independent and do things for yourself. It's a hard feeling to articulate, however when you don't know who you are, it's difficult to overlook. Getting to know yourself is difficult, however it's justified, despite all the trouble.

Always record the majority of your objectives that you feel have been accomplished and need to be accomplished. Moreover, record the occasions in your life that have happened, and that have formed or influenced you. At the point when life brings issues or incidents, it shapes our conviction framework and makes us think unexpectedly, however it makes us who we are. These things you rundown are naturally you, not a straightforward impression of society.

Many people are hated on and killed because of their personalities. In this day and time, teenagers are hustling to have flavor and drip sauce to show people that they're the better individual. When I say drip sauce, I'm pertaining to the word style. This isn't an activity in floundering. It's about details and recognizable proof of issues. These issues may keep you from achieving your present potential and letting your actual self bloom. Invest a little energy illuminating the past in your course of events. A course of events analysis is a fantastically targeted technique for discounting past events throughout your life that you consider being major. You look at them as development squares and as changing encounters along your course of events, without pervading them with an excessive amount of feeling. Keeping this written work a resume, keep it straightforward, and dense to the significant impacts or lessons gained from each past episode. At the point when you're breaking down negative past encounters, concentrate on what you gained from them. Everybody has these blips in their course of events. However, misrepresenting or overlooking them won't help you. Instead, perceive that these encounters molded you.

16

PERSONALITY

One of the most difficult things to express to the world, is that life is much better with God. The first step in finding this out is to give him a chance. Many people say our art and handwriting describe our personality. Many will agree and disagree in a variety of ways. The only person who fully understands our personality is God. Many people may be able to describe our personality, but it becomes quite difficult to breakdown every aspect. Our personality is used toward many things like job interviews, court rooms, trust, and pretty much everything. The difference between receiving a deal and not receiving a deal from someone is based on our personality.

One thing I acknowledged at an early age is the fact that finessing will only take you so far. No matter what the fact of the matter is, we as people can only pretend for so long. Many times we miss out on opportunities and good advice because of our impatience towards the communication. Negotiating properly usually benefits most situations. The way my personality was years ago helped me to connect with the right people I know today. My attitude, wisdom, sense of humor, emotions, and the way I dealt with negative things and people, have put me ahead. Brilliant people usually choose the route to stay neutral in various situations. Staying neutral is not always the best answer, but it's rarely ever a poor decision.

More than often, our personality will benefit us if we know our type. When somebody knows his or her style and invests some energy into understanding the elements of their identity, they rapidly turn out to be more veritable, compelling, and proficient. The more we learn about ourselves, the more we're able to discover happiness and a wonderful spouse. At the point when preparing to engage in work studies, groups start working better together in the matter of weeks. The difference this will create will help people that we're around daily. These enhancements are seen on all that really matters and in confidence.

In order to use confidence, we have to already believe in ourselves. Tolerating yourself and admiring who you are is important. You will see the best parts of yourself. Most individuals cherish their depiction and are pleased with who they are. Once we find ourselves, we find our peace, happiness, and gifts. Personalities are so beautiful that we can't draw them. Everybody participates the best when they are working with their inherent qualities. Working in our qualities additionally gives us vitality and pleasure. Pleasure is the most astonishing gift to use in any career or workforce. More like a coin, each identity sort of has a flip side. When you have qualities, then you have shortcomings. Working in our shortcomings channels our vitality and commonly causes disappointment.

When faced by a circumstance that hits our blind side, we normally talk and act in ways we wish to take back. Recognizing blind sides permits us to act intentionally as opposed to unknowingly when these circumstances happen. Blind spots are obstacles thrown out by the devil that we have to take time out of our day, to figure out how we can help ourselves without hurting ourselves. Picking a career that is fulfilling to you, whether it is the actual work or the workplace, is important. You can plant yourself where you will flourish instead of surviving. You will be able to grow better connections by turning out to be additionally understanding and tolerating of individuals who are not the same as you. However, it's not always a wise decision to connect yourself around people who have the same personality as you. Sometimes we have to acknowledge that enough of our gift is already been utilized. A variety of wonderful personalities will help many businesses rather than a variety of people with identical personalities. You can welcome their disparities when you perceive how their qualities and recognition can help you.

Our choice of words is usually going to determine the outcome of many situations. Our decision-making today will always affect the future. Failures more often than not get distracted in the moment. Personalities determine how people will deal with us and treat us. Great personalities usually will carry people a long way. The things we type, share, like, or comment on social media, determine the way people will judge us and deal with us. So many people begin to fail trying to satisfy the wrong individuals. No one wants to hire anyone or do business with someone in a professional field that's usually using foul language or negative thoughts on social media. We forget what's the most important and what we're living for.

17

IT'S NOT WHERE YOU FROM BUT WHERE YOU'RE HEADED

Growing up, I wanted to move away from my small town to a big city. As a kid, I remember telling individuals I don't want to be a millionaire, I just want to be successful. Over time my thoughts began to change and I recognized unique gifts that I didn't know I had. The indifference now is, I believe that just wanting to be successful is normal. Many people are shooting for the sky but not what's in the sky. Well, if I shoot further, maybe I will come in contact with a bigger target and my legacy will become bigger. The reason I'm not satisfied with just being successful is because I have generations behind me I have a responsibility to financially benefit, before they ever step foot on this earth.

Many individuals are satisfied with struggling and living paycheck to paycheck. There are also individuals who are satisfied with their career as long as it benefits them, without putting forth an effort to financially support the generations after them. When I leave the face of this Earth, I want to leave my family and friends financially happy. The other forms of happiness is usually something that they will have to obtain on their own. Most African Americans have less than fifteen thousand dollars in their savings account. This is not because they're dumb but because we're ignorant of a lot of things. Yes, many of us African Americans are very intelligent, but we're blind to a lot of things and are very lazy. We're actually satisfied with working for someone who decides our pay. The way our money is being taken away from our checks is very cruel to a human being. As long as we're working for someone, the more hours we put in at work equates to the more money that will be deducted from our checks.

In the community I grew up in, we weren't taught to start our own business. We were told that if we come to school late, we will one day arrive to work late and possibly get fired because our boss wouldn't tolerate it. Well, why doesn't the schoolhouse tell us we can be our own bosses? I come from a community where parents are buying their children Jordan shoes but not investing in them. Investing in your money is misunderstood in my community. Making money while on vacation is unreal in my community. Growing up, I was told if I didn't go to work, I wouldn't get paid. This thought can sometimes automatically keep a child from reaching their highest potential. When we don't profit, more, it can by one means or another simply run away over the span of our everyday lives, as we spend a little on this and a little on that. Rather than giving that a chance to transpire, however, consider spending some of your cash deliberately, by applying it in ways that can reinforce your money related condition or that can pay profits in different ways.

I was blessed with the knowledge to know that with my thoughts and views on life, I needed to place myself in a bigger city with bigger and better people. Much to my surprise, it actually worked out for me and benefited me a dozen different ways. Growing up in Fitzgerald, Georgia can either make or break a person. The biggest problem in my hometown is the ability for a young person to discover happiness and success. The vision there is dull, and it's very hard to acknowledge where you're going and how you're going to do it. There aren't many job opportunities, neither are their career opportunities that avoid going to college so you need that. It's not an awful place to raise a child because their chances are less likely of getting seriously hurt or worse. How can we find out where we're headed if we don't even know where we are?

People are caught up in what they drive instead of what drives them. It's not what a person thinks, but what they do. The things in life that genuinely matter are your family, your home, your interests and your profession. Everybody has one. Yours is as exceptional to you as your unique fingerprint, and is always showing signs of change. To find out where we are first, we need to discover a change immediately. Each new and energizing phase of life compels us to take a gander at our very own economies. Life became serious to me when I acknowledged the fact that there are as many tragedies as comedies.

Sometimes we set little mini goals and fail and think it's okay because nobody was watching or no one ever knew we were aiming for such a spot. The little goals that we fail at and postpone fixing reflect on bigger situations. We fail at things like staying on a diet, running a 5k, keeping a New Year's resolution, or controlling clutter in our homes. One thing football showed me about life was the fact that the little things mattered. Whenever we faced a team, which was an obstacle in our life, whoever did the little things right usually won the game. We fail in the larger things like overcoming an addiction, finding employment, or holding on to an important relationship. At times, our peers get lost in the moment of life and forget the blessings they have and worry about what they don't have.

Sometimes these same failures negatively impact the rest of our lives like keeping a marriage together, persuading a child to make better choices, or overcoming a lifetime of debt. Failure is very necessary, we couldn't be successful without it. Sometimes we become comfortable with failure because we know many others are also experiencing it. A lot of times we are uncertain about whether or not we should give up on a situation. The thing is, if I'm experiencing more failure than success after a long period of time, I will let the project go. Maybe you won't be at the top, but we should all expect to move forward when we're pursuing a project. At the point when disappointment happens, which it generally will, the smartest of us trip internally to decide the cause and purposeful strides we can take to gain from the experience. Also, in time, we figure out how to champion modesty.

A standout amongst the most trust filled minutes in life is the point at which we discover the boldness to relinquish what we can't change. The things we can't change are where we grew up, where we're from, what we've been through, and more. The things we can change are where we're going. Each and every one of us needs someone in our life, no matter how much we think we don't. No one effectively explores life alone. At the point when the trust inside us starts to blur, we search for it in others. We swing to family. On the chance that family is not accessible, we swing to companions. What's more, if companions are not accessible, we search for purposeful groups around us to discover support.

18

TAEYLON GAULDEN-HODGE
MY STORY

My life has been pretty charming for the last 19 years. I've utilized ups and downs all the way around. Before I could even remember, I began to love football with a passion. I love to do simple math problems without pen and paper. I was pretty awesome at the things I loved. Those things fulfilled my life, my happiness, and my self-esteem.

One thing about all the talent we receive is that I believe we can use them all in one. The neighborhood I grew up in wasn't extremely dangerous, but there were negative things within my neighborhood that I was attached to.

When I was about seven or eight, I would walk outside to play football and see dope dealers walk by. As days flew by, I became familiar with some of those faces and names, and soon we knew each other. Most of them were older than me, and I learned a lot from them.

I wasn't sure if I should be like them or play football, since my father was a part of both. I knew for sure I wanted to be a football player with no doubts about it. The lifestyle we see when we look out our blinders can either be motivation or a downfall.

I picture myself in the hood with my friends and I pictured myself playing sports with my friends. The thing I realized at a very young age was that one of them will end sooner than the other if I'm not careful. One thing I can honestly say is from a little boy to a teenager, I took every day of my life a day at a time. There were times I reacted too fast because of my impatience, and there have been times I've reacted too slowly.

My dreams have become much bigger than average.

My dreams became bigger the more I work. The more I work, the more I find the love and the enthusiasm to become even better.

There haven't been many obstacles in my way that I've been stuck on. I would always find a bridge to walk over or under. Parts of my family, coming from my mother's and my father's family, helped me with their choice of actions. There are those who had always been positive and consistent with their work, which have enabled them to be able to afford nice things. I have family that have been average most of their lives and those who have been struggling. I received enough support to maintain a stable mindset.

The roads I've traveled and the hills I've climbed have been preparing me for success. I was the only man in my household for the majority of my life, but it came with the good and the bad. For the most part, my grandfather was always the father figure of my life. He showed me the ways of being a man before anything.

My grandfather was my first coach throughout my favorite sport. There were things he'd seen in me more than any coach that knew me afterwards, but of course it would be difficult for him to help them do their job when he's not a part of the staff.

I was told by many that I was a million-dollar football player. The way I set my dreams up, there wasn't a second in my life when I didn't think I would not play football after high school.

Maybe I was a little too sure, but hey life goes on, so why shouldn't I?

There have been many days in my life where I completely hid my feelings and my way of thinking. Many days after high school practices and games, I would see players get handed letters from different universities. The thing that bothered me most, was the fact that I was a dominant player or a key player. Every day I walked into the locker room, I prayed for a letter. I even accomplished things like leading the team in rushing yards and touchdowns my junior year for one of the best schools in the state of Georgia. I went out of my way and took different avenues to get different schools to accept me on their field.

The summer after I graduated, I traveled to Georgia military college in Milledgeville, Georgia to try out for their team. I feel that I did a great job while being at the camp. My biggest downfall at the football camps was that I was not very fast, or quick, and could hardly jump. However, on the football field, I could play just as good as one of the greatest. I'm the kid that you just have to hand a helmet and pads to in order to see if I'm really talented.

I ended up not attending school at Georgia military college after failing to make the team. I began school at Georgia Perimeter College in Atlanta during the upcoming fall semester. I failed again because I was in a rush to hop on someone's football field, so I immediately changed schools during the upcoming winter semester and ended up at Morehouse University. The things I planned to pursue at Morehouse University didn't work out either. Life goes on and the greatest thing I've done since I've graduated was to move along with those things.

I grew up in a household with a single parent and one little sister. When I graduated, it was my time to escape the little town I was in because I knew there was nothing for me but a greater opportunity for me to fail.

The hard thing about leaving was the fact that there was no other man in my house that had been there for them like me. In fact, it was one of the hardest decisions I've ever made in my life. I ended up having a discussion with God, and he told me you will fail at many things again and again, while you're away, but you will walk out of the fire and will open many eyes and you will be able to do anything for your mother and sister.

I watched my mom struggle physically and mentally my entire life but, on the outside looking in, people couldn't tell. If my mom didn't know how to do anything, she could paint a pretty picture for nosey people.

The difference between my future and my past is that I have another opportunity to do things differently. Without a past there is no future. I do not base my future upon my past, however many things in my future will cause me to ponder my past.

I've learned each day is an opportunity to improve as a leader. I seek strategies that keep me from saying, "I wish I knew back then what I know now."

Life is a gamble and so are our day-to-day choices. My past was a teaching session while my future is a test. Life isn't based on being perfect, it's based on gaining from the things and individuals we've experienced. My future will contrast my past, since I've adapted alternative courses and strategies to finish an assortment of things.

Every day is a chance for a brighter future. The obstacles I've run into along the way have prepared me for upcoming events and tragedies.

Life is a gamble and death is a guarantee.